A MODERN METHOD FOR GUITAR SCALES

Larry Baione

BERKLEE PRESS
Editor in Chief: Jonathan Feist
Senior Vice President of Online Learning and Continuing Education/CEO of Berklee Online: Debbie Cavalier
Vice President of Enrollment Marketing and Management: Mike King
Vice President of Online Education: Carin Nuernberg
Editorial Assistants: Emily Jones, Eloise Kelsey, Megan Richardson
Cover Design: Ranya Karafilly

ISBN 978-1-4950-7717-3

1140 Boylston Street
Boston, MA 02215-3693 USA
(617) 747-2146

Visit Berklee Press Online at
www.berkleepress.com

DISTRIBUTED BY

7777 W. BLUEMOUND RD. P.O. BOX 13819
MILWAUKEE, WISCONSIN 53213

Visit Hal Leonard Online
www.halleonard.com

Berklee Press, a publishing activity of Berklee College of Music, is a not-for-profit educational publisher.
Available proceeds from the sales of our products are contributed to the scholarship funds of the college.

CONTENTS

PREFACE

Welcome to *A Modern Method for Guitar Scales*. Why practice scales? Here are a few reasons:

- It helps you learn your instrument.
- It helps you organize and understand the guitar fingerboard.
- It helps you to develop your technique and your sound.
- It helps you play melodies and improvise.
- It helps you to read on the instrument, and eventually sight-read.
- It improves your command of the guitar.

This book shows the fingerings that I learned from the great guitar teacher, William Leavitt, the author of the *A Modern Method for Guitar* series.

The scale fingerings presented in this book will help you learn the fingerboard of this beautiful instrument. If you play some scales with different fingerings, please add the fingerings presented here to your repertoire. One key to playing the guitar musically is making the appropriate choice in fingering of a phrase—the choice for it to be played with the best control.

I wish you great success in your playing and performing on the guitar.

—Larry Baione, Boston, MA

CHAPTER 1

Major

W W H W W W H

The major scale is a seven-note scale with the whole-step/half-step pattern: W W H W W W H. A whole step is the distance two frets apart; a half step is on the adjacent fret.

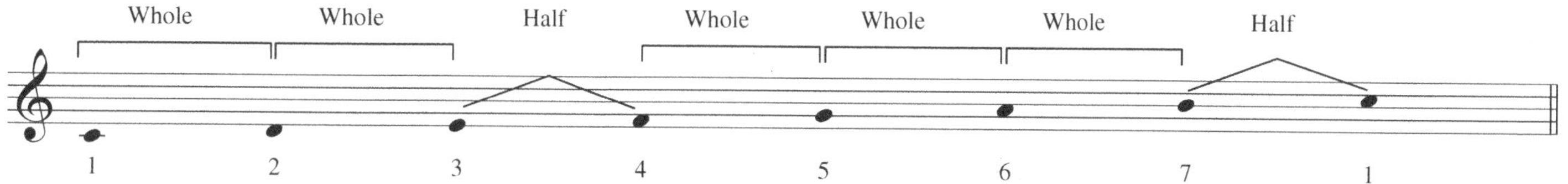

FIG. 1.1. C Major Scale

Often, other scales are described in terms of how they relate to the major scale. We will use it to illustrate various concepts throughout this book, which you can then apply to other scales.

FINGERING TYPES

There are many ways to play any scale (in a specific octave) on the guitar—both within a single position and at different frets. *Fingering types* are movable patterns that include all the notes of a scale, and by moving them to different frets, different scales can be performed.

Figure 1.2 is a fingering type diagram—in this case, for major-scale fingering type I. Here, the pattern is set in the second position, where it covers the notes of C major (and thus, all the modes of C major). Note the following components of the fingering type diagram:

1. Horizontal lines represent guitar strings. The high E string is on top; the low E string is on the bottom.
2. Numerals indicate left-hand fingerings: 1 for index, 2 for middle finger, 3 for ring finger, and 4 for pinky.

3. A circled numeral indicates the lowest root of the scale. In figure 1.2, where we specify that the fingering is for the C major scale in position 2, the circled 2 indicates the note C (on the fifth string, 3rd fret, played by the 2nd finger).
4. The gray fret indicates the position (fret 2 in this case), which clarifies finger stretches outside the position.

As you can see, all *diatonic* (i.e., "of the scale") notes in the position are indicated in the diagram, which will span the position's two octaves plus a minor third (or plus a perfect fourth, for types that include finger stretches outside the position, marked FS). Figure 1.2 presents a fingering chart in its usual form, then an annotated version showing string names and notes instead of fingering numerals, and then the corresponding notation.

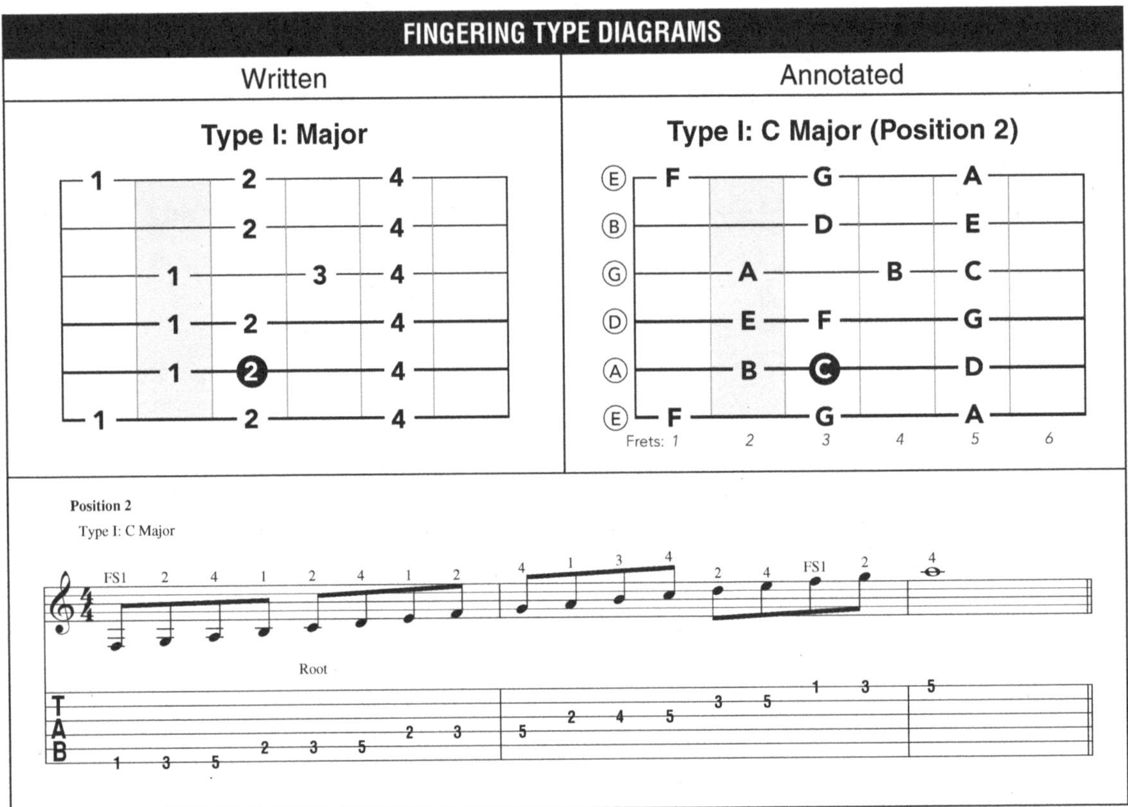

FIG. 1.2. Fingering Type I. As presented and annotated, relating to notes of the C Major scale in 2nd position.

Each fingering type is movable throughout the fretboard, similar to movable chord forms. So, as we have seen, in 2nd position, major-scale fingering type I includes the notes diatonic to a C major scale. In 3rd position, fingering type I covers notes diatonic to the C♯ (or D♭) major scale. Similarly, in 2nd position, major-scale fingering type II yields notes diatonic to G, rather than C (as in type I). Later in the chapter, we will see examples of these relationships between fingering types, positions, and keys.

First, let's explore the most useful fingering types for the major scales. As you can see, within a position, each fingering type covers notes of different major scales.

Here are all the major-scale fingering types. We will then look at them individually.

MAJOR-SCALE FINGERING TYPES

Type I: Major

1 2 4
2 4
1 3 4
1 2 4
1 ❷ 4
1 2 4

Type IA: Major

1 2 4
2 4
1 2 4
1 2 4
1 2 4
❶ 2 4

Type II: Major

1 2 4
2 4
1 3 4
1 3 4
1 2 4
1 ❷ 4

Type III: Major

1 2 4
1 2 4
1 3
1 3 4
1 3 ❹
1 2 4

Type IV: Major

1 3 4
1 2 4
1 3
1 3 4
1 3 4
1 3 ❹

FIG. 1.3. Major Scale Fingering Types

Type I Major-Scale Fingering: Two First-Finger Stretches

Type I fingering includes two stretches for the first finger, reaching to the first fret.

Type I: Major

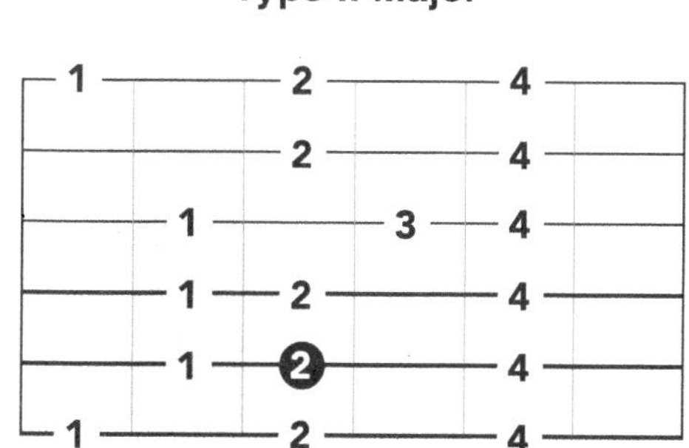

FIG. 1.4. Type I Fingering for Major Scales

Type IA Major-Scale Fingering: Three First-Finger Stretches

Type IA fingering is a variation of type I, but it includes an additional first-finger stretch, as well as a different fingering on the third string.

Type IA: Major

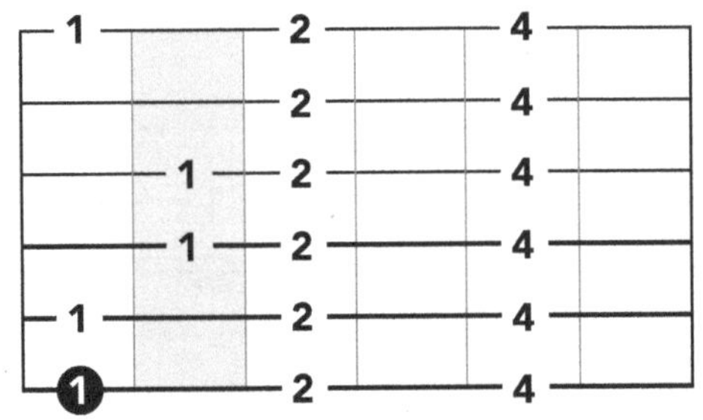

FIG. 1.5. Type IA Fingering for Major Scales

Type II Major-Scale Fingering: No Stretches

Type II fingering for the major scale does not require any finger stretches.

Type II: Major

1 2 4
2 4
1 3 4
1 3 4
1 2 4
1 2 4

FIG. 1.6. Type II Fingering Diagram for Major Scales

Type III Major-Scale Fingering: No Stretches

Type III fingering is also free from finger stretches.

Type III: Major

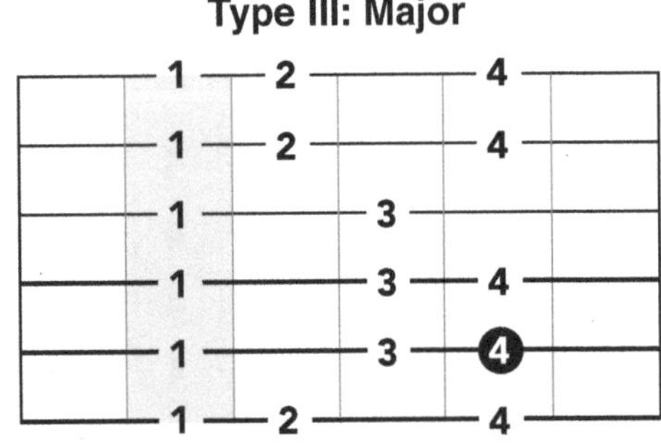

FIG. 1.7. Type III Fingering for G Major Scale (7th Position)

Type IV Major-Scale Fingering: One Fourth-Finger Stretch

In *type IV fingering* for major scales, the fourth-finger stretches.

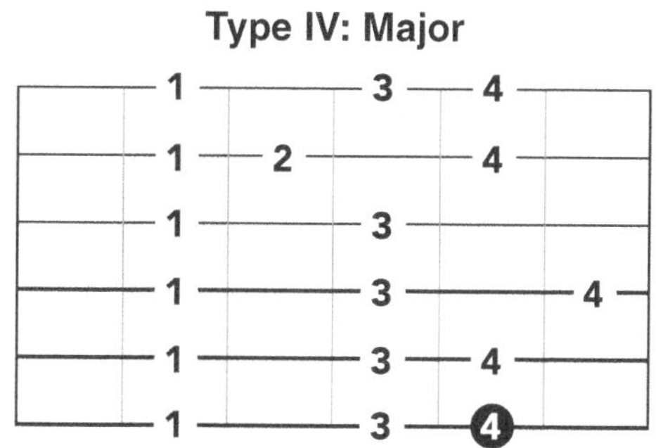

FIG. 1.8. Type IV Fingering for Major Scales

This chart shows the scales yielded by the different fingering types through 12th position. (Not all the notes are possible in first position, without playing open strings.)

MAJOR SCALES (FINGERING TYPES)	POSITIONS 1	2	3	4	5	6	7	8	9	10	11	12
I Two First-Finger Stretches	(B)	C	C♯	D	E♭	E	F	F♯	G	A♭	A	B♭
IA Three First-Finger Stretches	(E)	F	F♯	G	A♭	A	B♭	B	C	C♯	D	E♭
II No Stretches	F♯	G	A♭	A	B♭	B	C	C♯	D	E♭	E	F
III No Stretches	C♯	D	E♭	E	F	F♯	G	A♭	A	B♭	B	C
IV One Fourth-Finger Stretch	A♭	A	B♭	B	C	C♯	D	E♭	E	F	F♯	G

FIG. 1.9. Major-Scale Fingering Types, Positions, and Tonics

RANGE STUDIES

Practice major scales throughout the full range of your guitar, using all five fingering types for each key. Start on the root, then go as high and as low as you can go while staying in position (except for any stretches that are part of the fingering type). Shown is C major, in all five fingering types, but adapt it to all keys, referencing the chart in figure 1.9, as necessary.

Use a metronome. Start slowly, and gradually increase the tempo. Also try repeating each note, using alternate picking or other picking patterns. Then create your own similar exercises using other major scales and other positions.

FIG. 1.10. Major-Scale Range Studies

Three-Octave Fingerings

In addition to playing scales using the fingering types, which are based on positions, practice them in three octaves, changing positions and using open strings as necessary.

FIG. 1.11. Major-Scale Three-Octave Fingering

POSITION STUDIES

In each position, practice all five major-scale fingering types, identifying each scale covered by each fingering type. Figure 1.12 presents the scales in positions 2, 5, and 7. Start with those, but continue through all positions. Use the chart in figure 1.9 as needed.

Position 5

Type I: E♭ Major

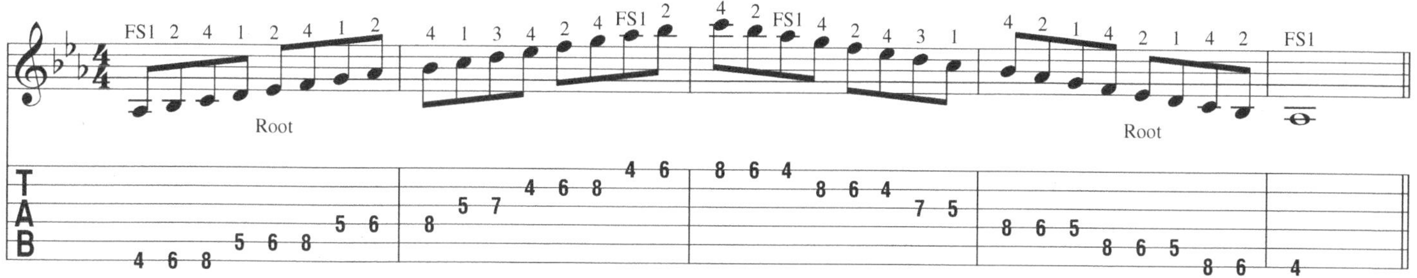

Type IA: A♭ Major

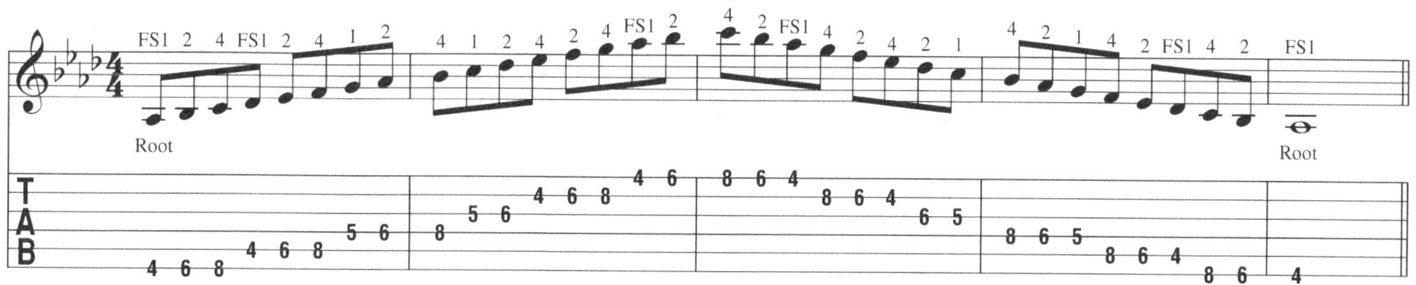

Type II: B♭ Major

Type III: F Major

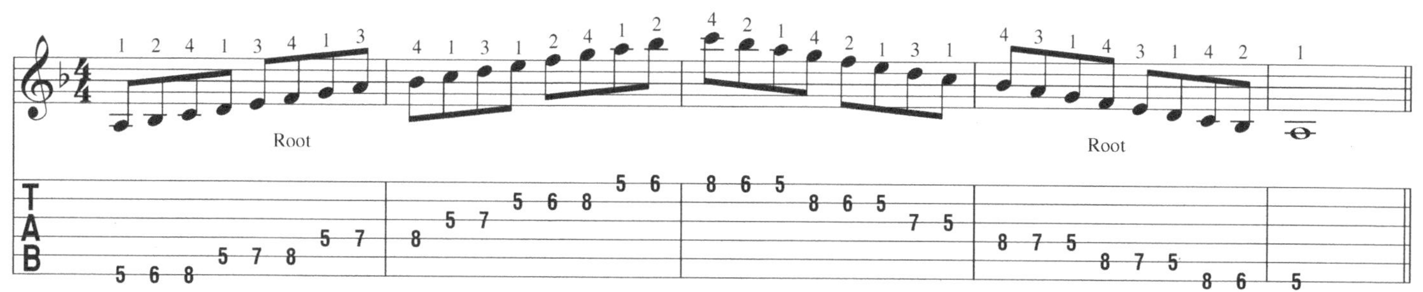

Type IV: C Major

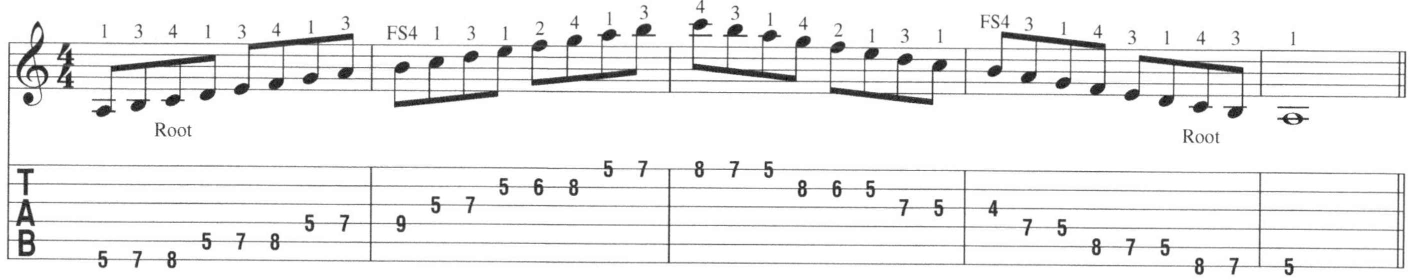

FIG. 1.12. Position Studies

TRANSPOSITION

Practice the major scale ascending and descending, in one octave and two octaves, in every key. Use all of the major-key fingering types.

FIG. 1.13. Major Scale Transposed to All Keys

ETUDES

B♭ Major Etude

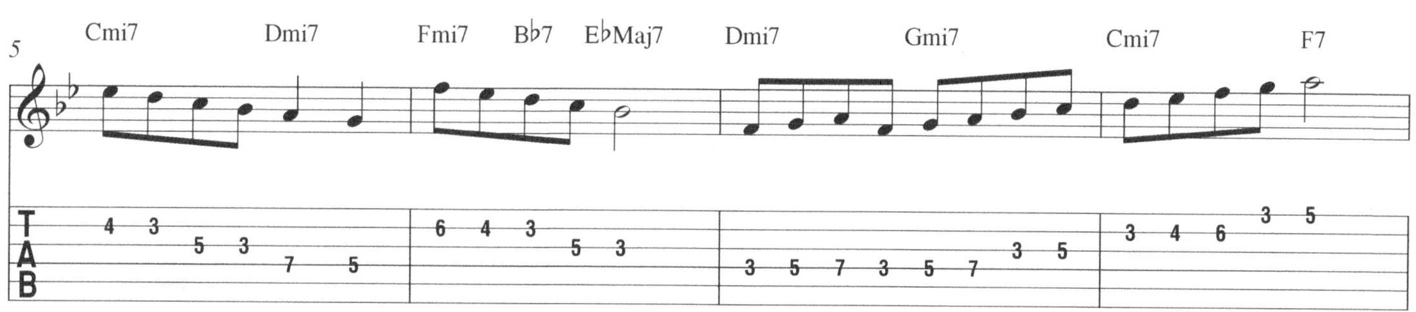

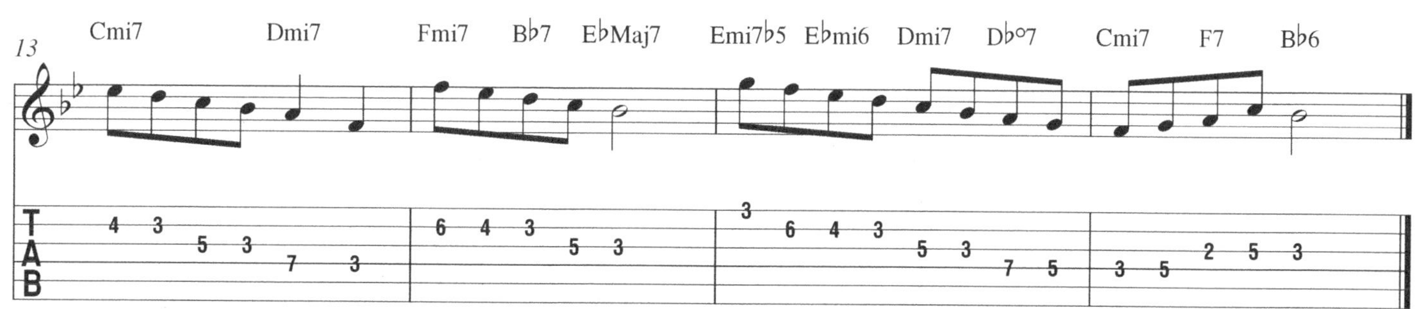

FIG. 1.14. Major-Scale Etude

C Major Etude

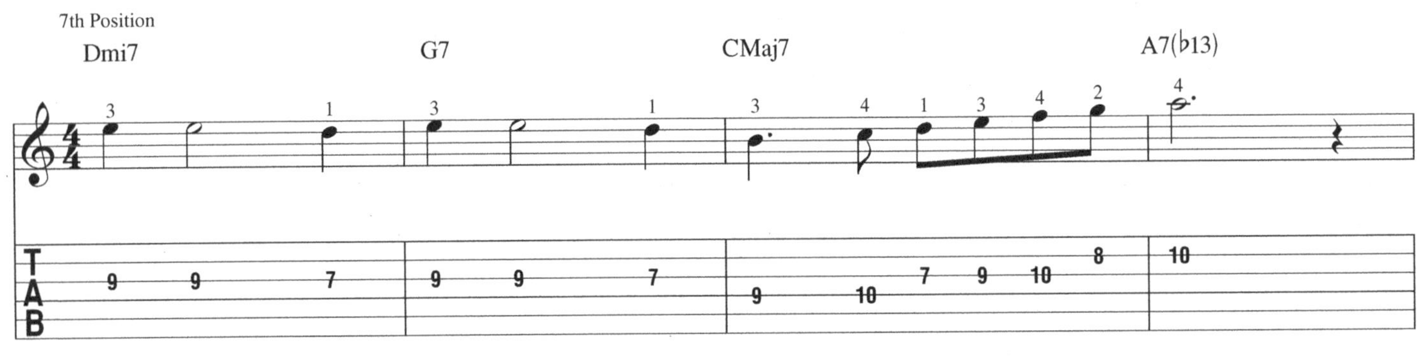

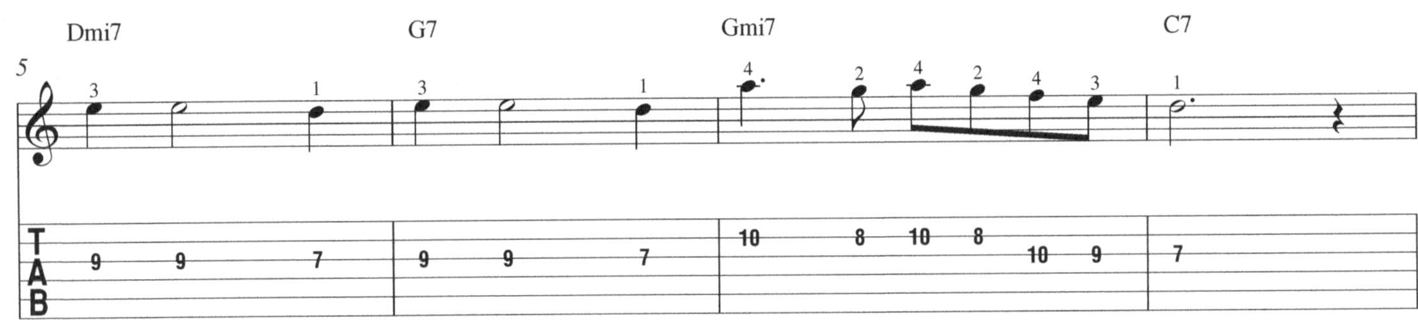

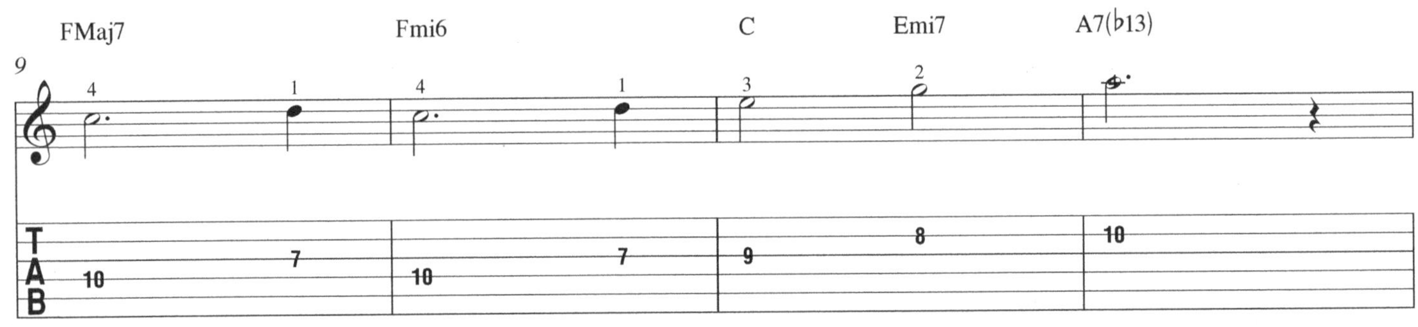

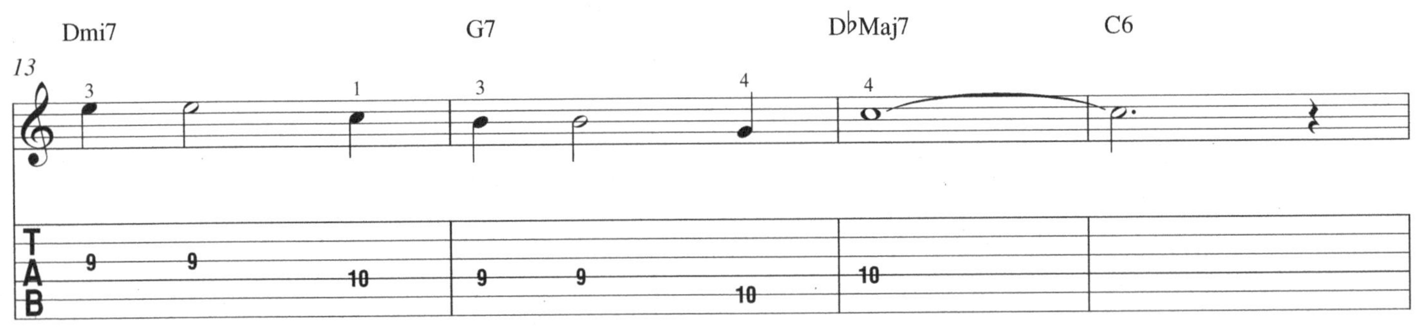

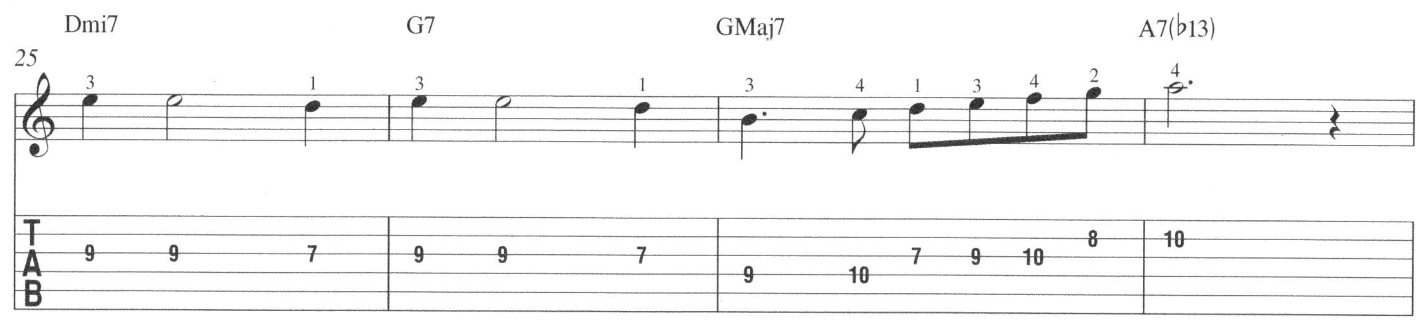

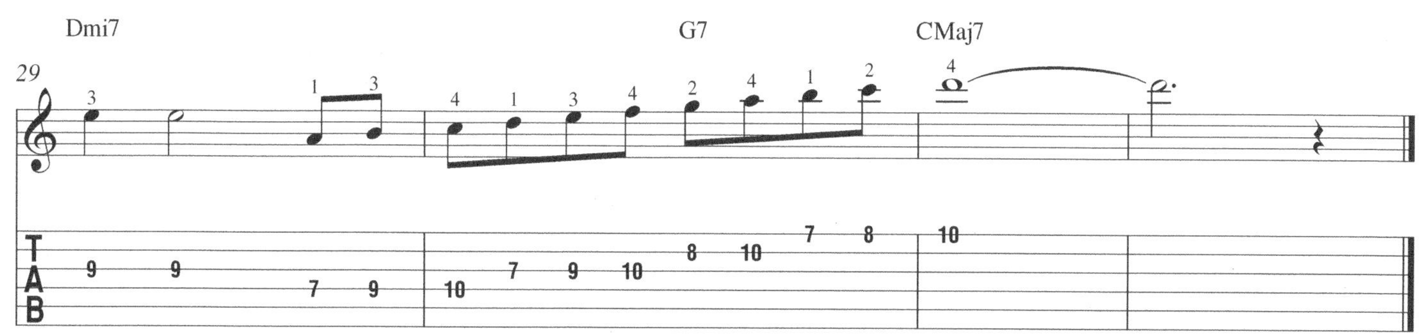

FIG. 1.15. C Major Etude

G Major Etude

FIG. 1.16. G Major Etude

F Major Etude

FIG. 1.17. F Major Etude

CHAPTER 2

Major Pentatonic

W W m3 W m3

The pentatonic scales are five-note scales. Major pentatonic is based on the major scale, omitting the 4 and 7, and leaving the notes 1 2 3 5 6. The step pattern between notes is W W m3 W m3.

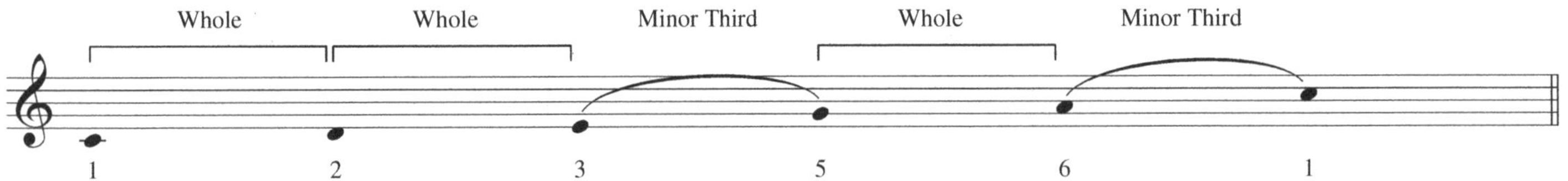

FIG. 2.1. C Major Pentatonic Scale

FINGERINGS

There are three common fingering types for major pentatonic. Notice that they are similar to the major-scale fingering types, but with fewer notes. All three lay fully within position, without any stretches.

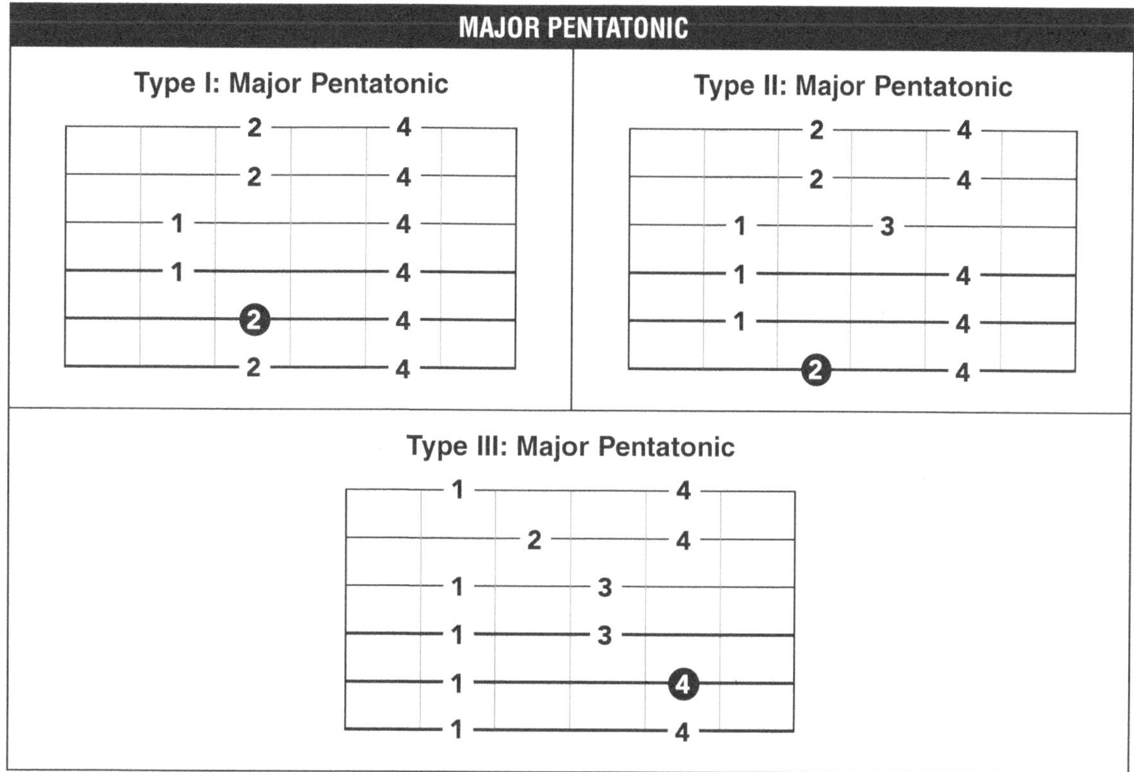

FIG. 2.2. Fingering Types for Major Pentatonic

This chart shows the most useful fingering types for major pentatonic, with the keys in positions 1 through 12.

MAJOR PENTATONICS		POSITIONS											
		1	2	3	4	5	6	7	8	9	10	11	12
FINGERING TYPES	I	B	C	C♯	D	E♭	E	F	F♯	G	A♭	A	B♭
	II	F♯	G	A♭	A	B♭	B	C	C♯	D	E♭	E	F
	III	C♯	D	E♭	E	F	F♯	G	A♭	A	B♭	B	C

FIG. 2.3. Major-Pentatonic Fingering Types, Positions, and Tonics

RANGE STUDIES

Practice major pentatonic scales throughout the full range of your guitar, in all three fingering types. C major is shown, but transpose this exercise for all other major pentatonic scales.

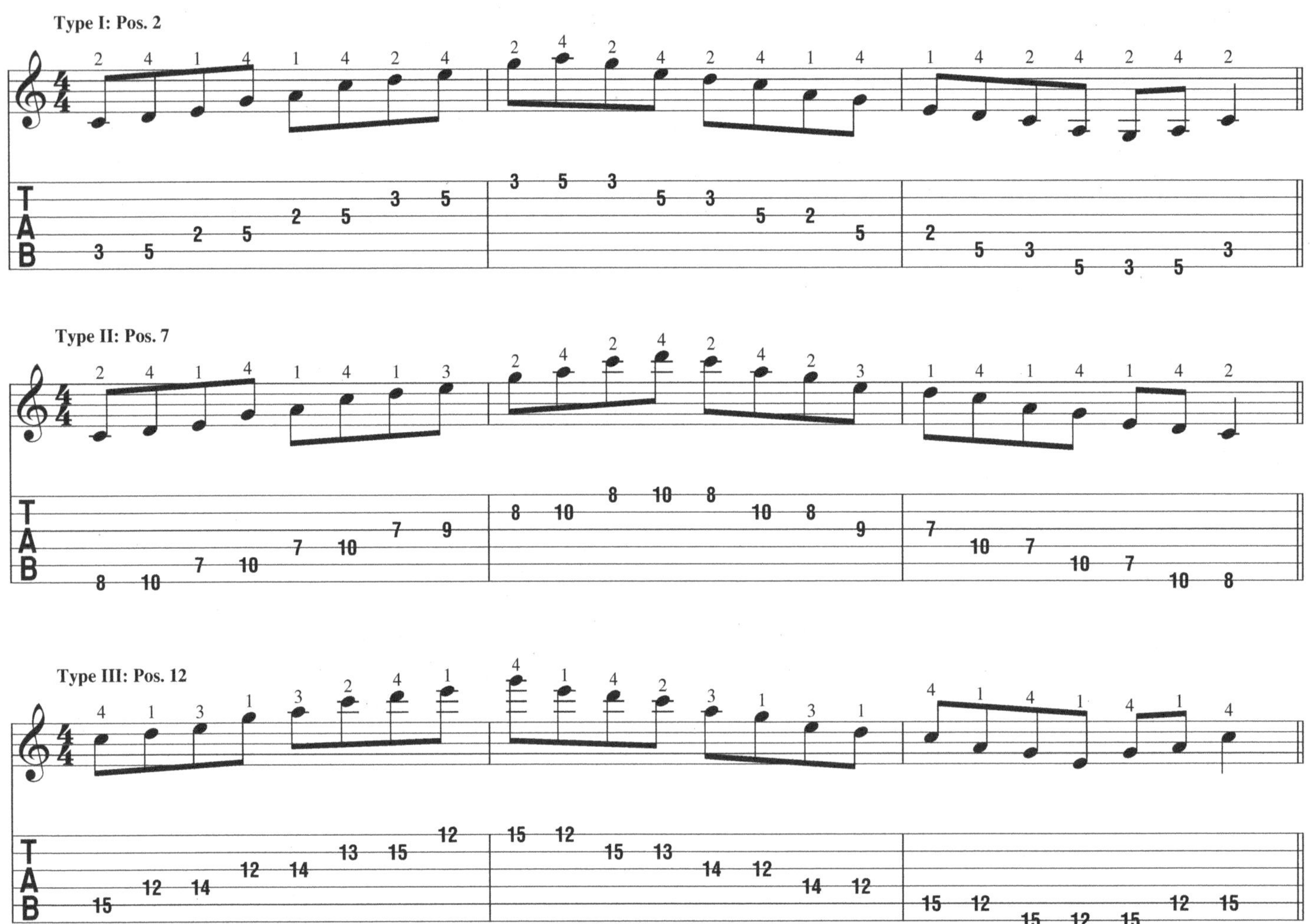

FIG. 2.4. C Major Pentatonic Range Study

POSITION STUDIES

Position 2

Type I: C Major Pentatonic

Type II: G Major Pentatonic

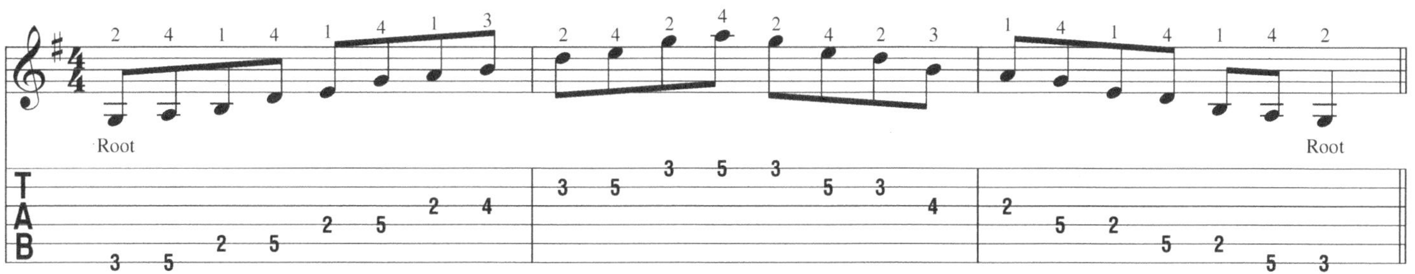

Type III: D Major Pentatonic

Position 5

Type I: E♭ Major Pentatonic

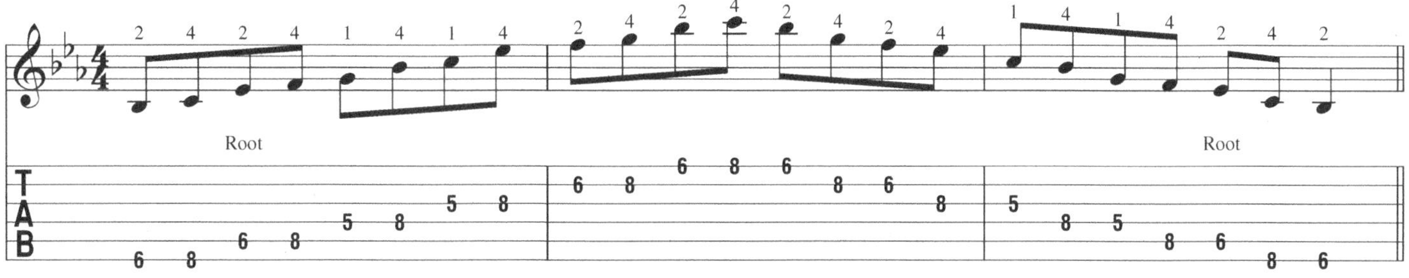

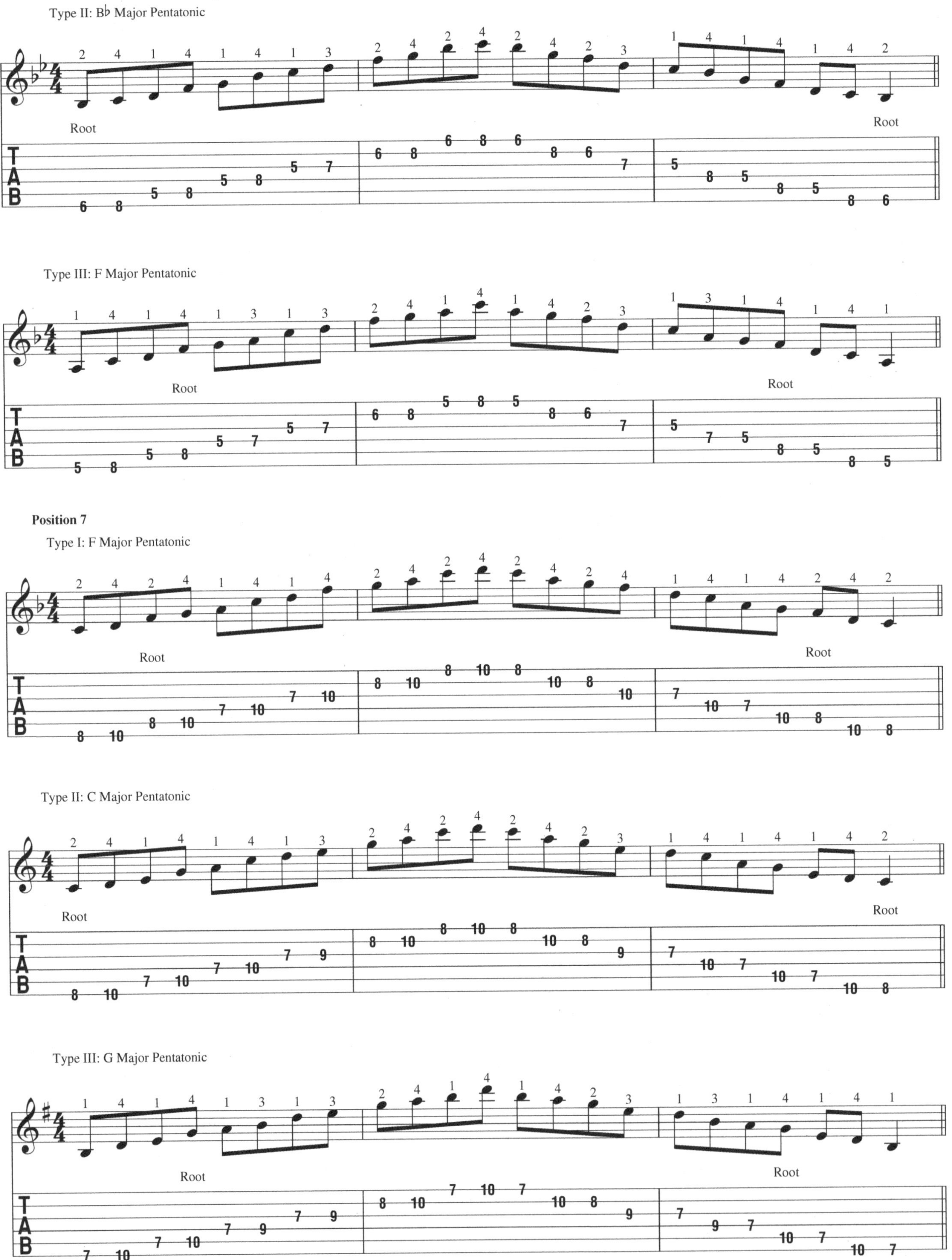

FIG. 2.5. Major Pentatonic Position Studies

TRANSPOSITION

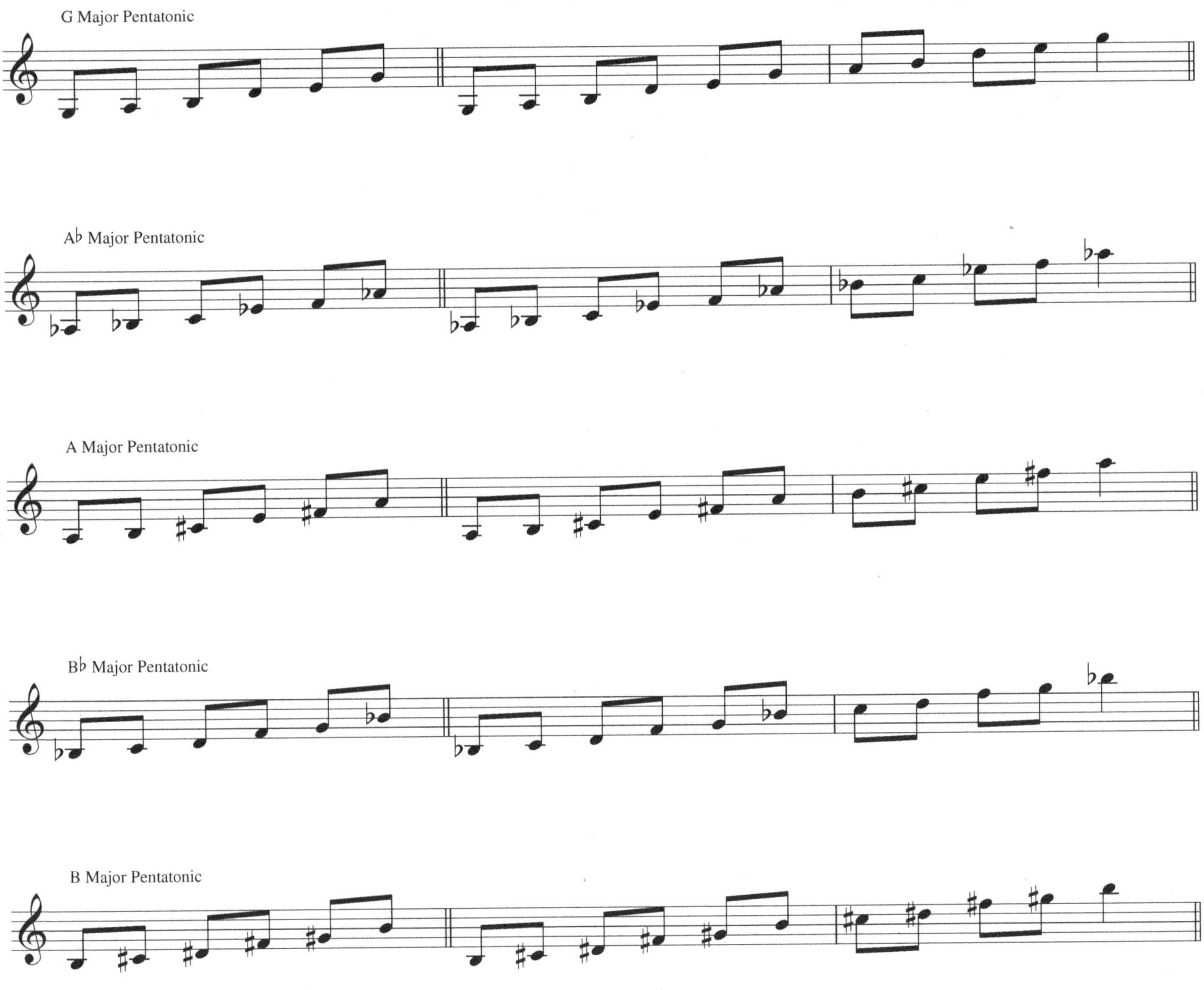

FIG. 2.6. Major Pentatonic in All Keys

ETUDE

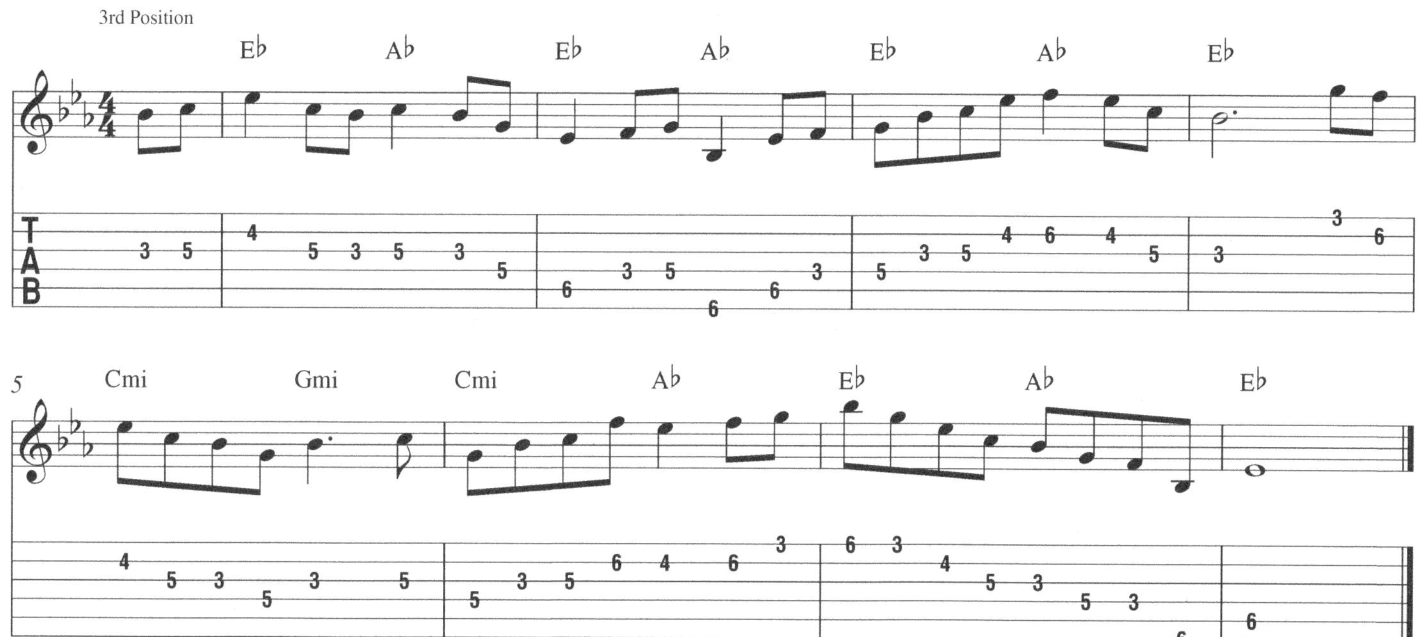

FIG. 2.7. Pentatonic Etude in 3rd Position

CHAPTER 3

Minor Pentatonic

m3 W W m3 W

The minor pentatonic scale is a five-note scale, with notes in the pattern m3 W W m3 W.

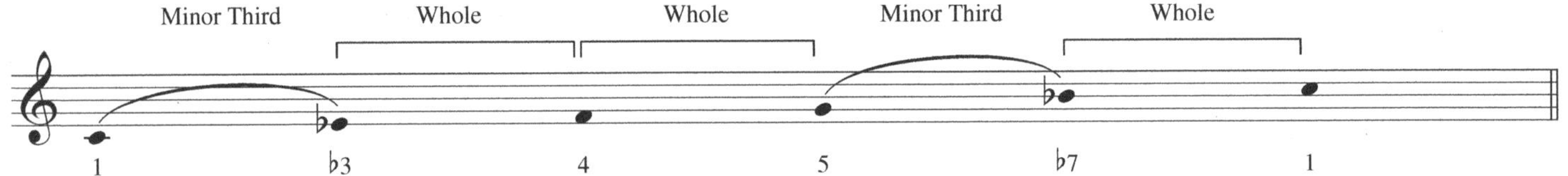

FIG. 3.1. C Minor Pentatonic Scale

FINGERING TYPES

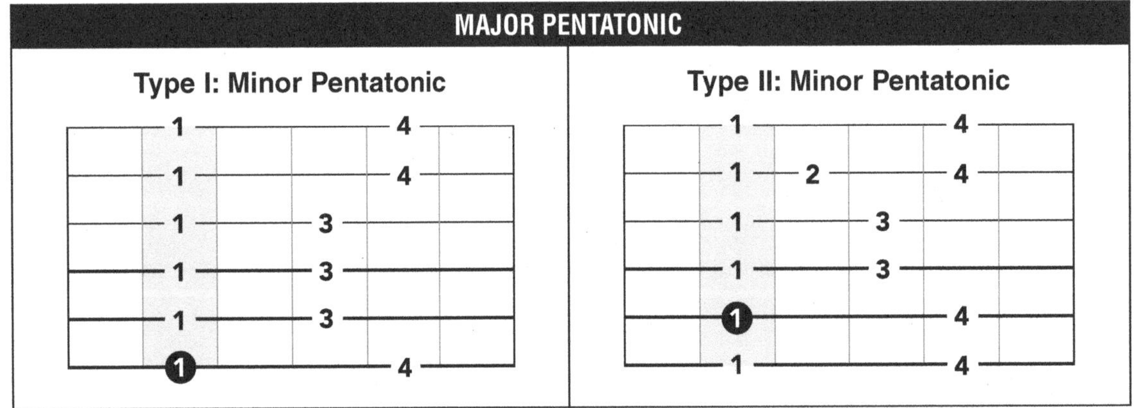

FIG. 3.2. Fingering Types for Minor Pentatonic

MINOR PENTATONIC SCALES		POSITIONS											
		1	2	3	4	5	6	7	8	9	10	11	12
FINGERING TYPES	I	F	F♯	G	A♭	A	B♭	B	C	C♯	D	E♭	E
	II	B♭	B	C	C♯	D	E♭	E	F	F♯	G	A♭	A

FIG. 3.3. Minor-Pentatonic Fingering Types, Positions, and Tonics

RANGE STUDIES

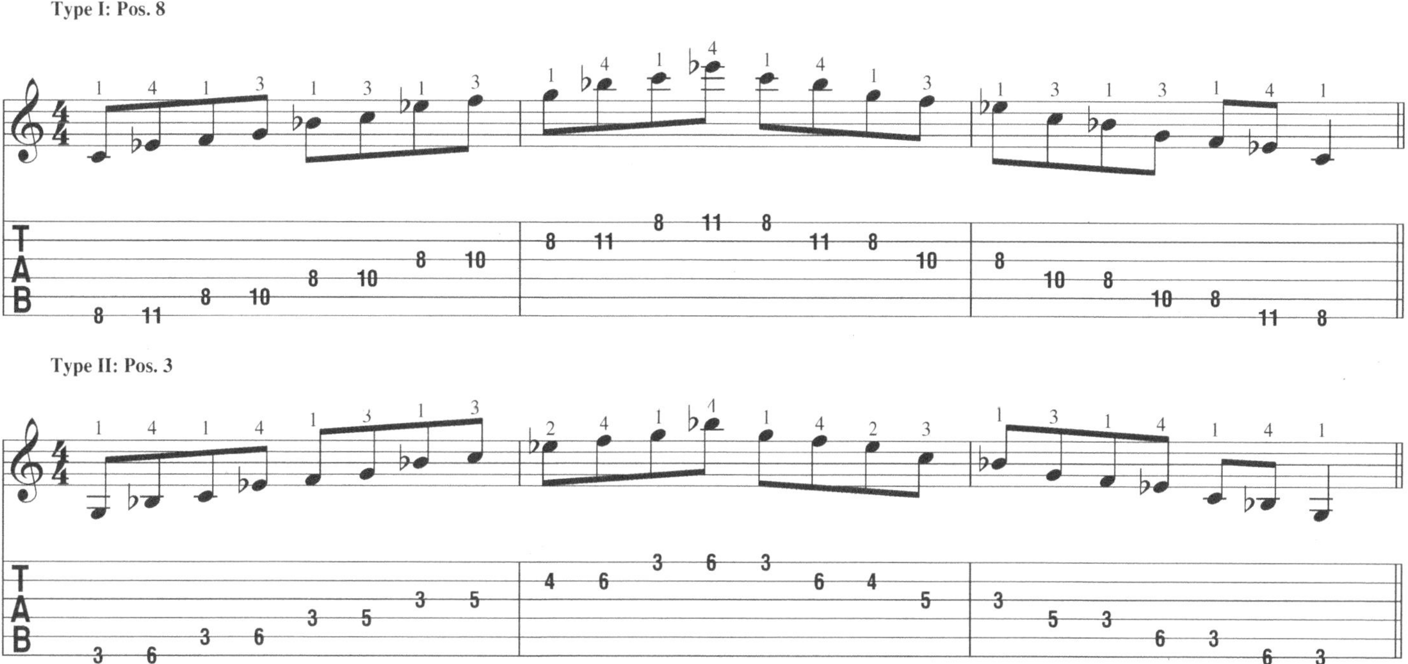

FIG. 3.4. Range Studies for Minor Pentatonic

POSITION STUDIES

FIG. 3.5. Position Studies

TRANSPOSITION

FIG. 3.6. Minor Pentatonic in All Keys

ETUDE

FIG. 3.7. A Minor Pentatonic Etude

CHAPTER 4

Blues

m3 W H H m3 W

The most common blues scale is like a pentatonic scale with an added half step between the 4 and 5, in the pattern: m3 W H H m3 W. The ♭5 "blue note" is the characteristic pitch.

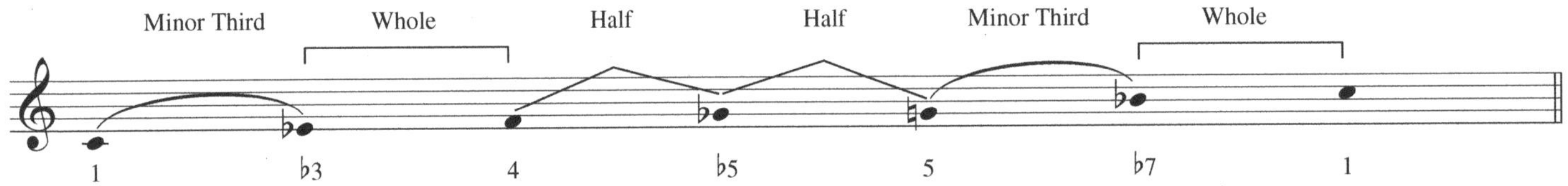

FIG. 4.1. C Blues Scale

FINGERINGS

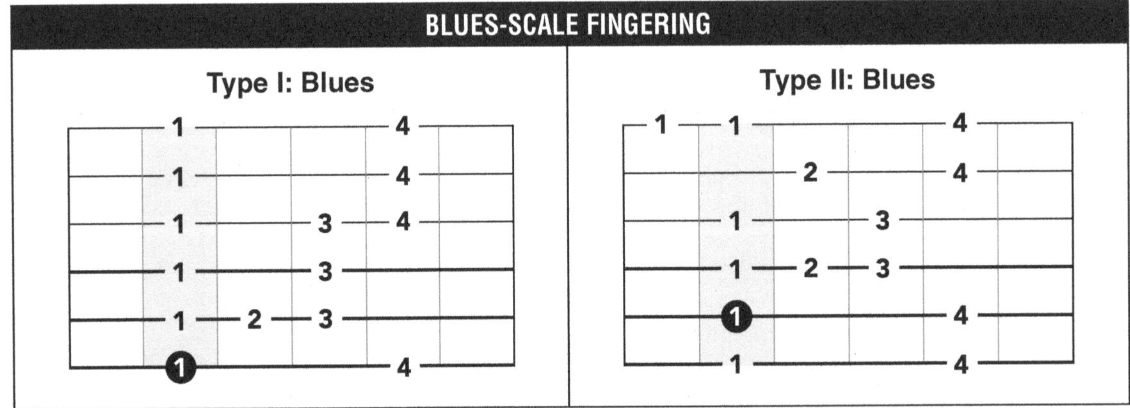

FIG. 4.2. Fingering Types for the Blues Scale

BLUES SCALES		POSITIONS											
		1	2	3	4	5	6	7	8	9	10	11	12
FINGERING TYPES	I	F	F♯	G	A♭	A	B♭	B	C	C♯	D	E♭	E
	II	B♭	B	C	C♯	D	E♭	E	F	F♯	G	A♭	A

FIG. 4.3. Blues Fingering Types, Positions, and Tonics

RANGE STUDIES

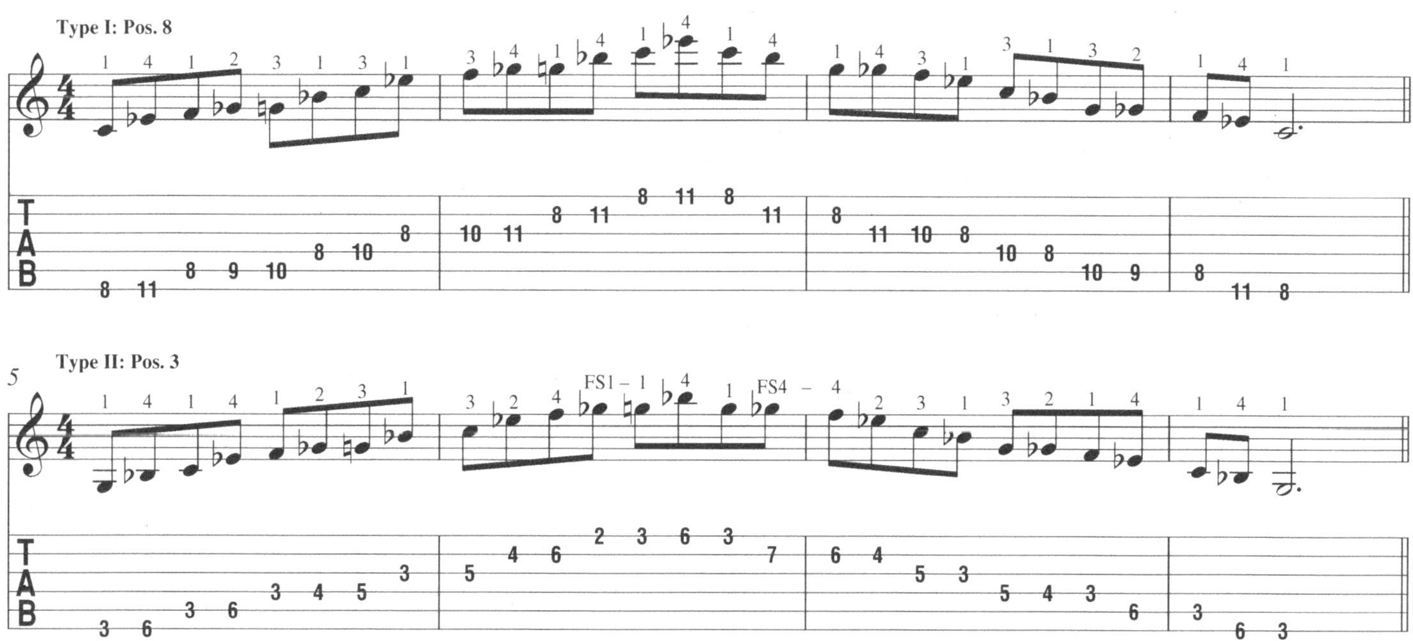

FIG. 4.4. Range Studies for C Blues

POSITION STUDIES

FIG. 4.5. Position Studies for Blues

TRANSPOSITION

FIG. 4.6. All Transpositions of the Blues Scale

ETUDES

F Blues Etude

FIG. 4.7. F Blues Etude

C Blues Etude

FIG. 4.8. C Blues Etude

CHAPTER 5

Modes

W W H W W W H

There are two common ways to discuss modes: as parallel variations of the major scale (e.g., C Dorian is like C major, but with a ♭3 and ♭7), and as displaced relative versions of a parent scale (e.g., D Dorian is diatonic to C major, starting on the 2nd degree).

Parallel modes share the same root (e.g., C major and C Dorian), but their other notes may be nondiatonic to each other's key. *Relative modes* share the same diatonic notes as a parent scale, starting on a different scale degree (e.g., C major and D Dorian).

When discussing modes as displaced scales, the modes include the same notes (and key) as the original parent scale, but starting on another scale degree. While any type of scale can have modes, in this chapter, we are concerned with modes of the major scale. Since there are seven degrees in a major scale, it has seven modes, each starting on a different degree. Notice that the pattern of whole and half steps remains intact, though shifting with each scale degree.

- *Ionian* starts on the 1: W w h w w w h. It is the same as the major scale, and one of the most commonly used scales.
- *Dorian* starts on the 2: w h w w w h W. It is like a major scale with a ♭3 and ♭7.
- *Phrygian* starts on the 3: h w w w h W w. It is like a major scale with ♭2, ♭3, ♭6, and ♭7.
- *Lydian* starts on the 4: w w w h W w h. It is like a major scale with a ♯4.
- *Mixolydian* starts on the 5: w w h W w h w. It is like a major scale with a ♭7.
- *Aeolian* starts on the 6: w h W w h w w. It is like major with ♭3, ♭6, and ♭7. It is also called the relative minor of the parent scale, or a natural minor scale. It is one of the most commonly used scales.
- *Locrian* starts on the 7: h W w h w w w. It is like a major scale with a ♭2, ♭3, ♭5, ♭6, and ♭7. While few tunes are completely based on Locrian, it is useful for improvising on the mi7♭5 chord.

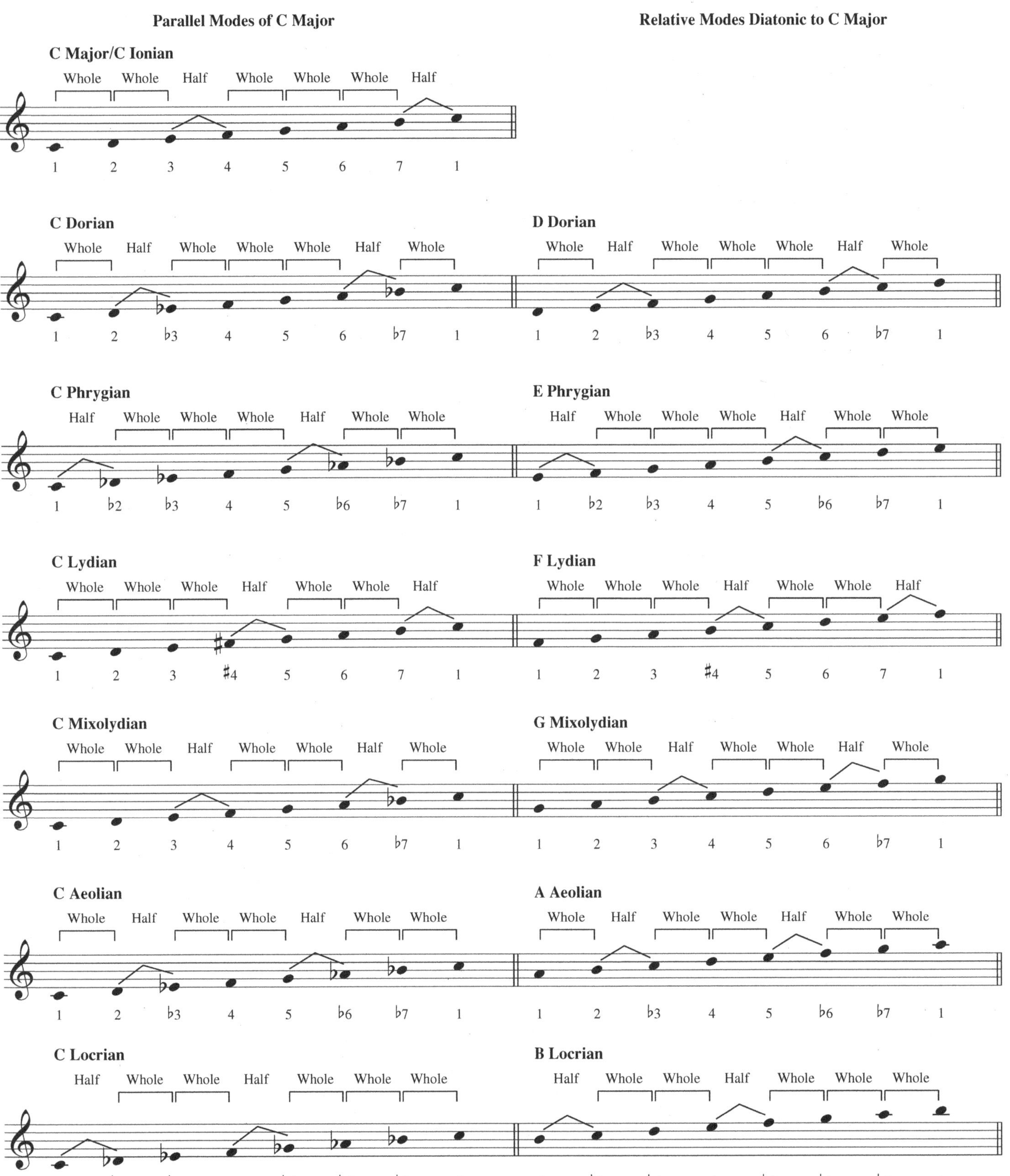

FIG. 5.1. Parallel and Relative Modes

Both ways of describing modes may seem derivative. In practice, each mode has its own distinct color and effect. While from a technical perspective, the modes share commonalities in construction and thus in fingering, they should be studied independently for their unique characters.

FINGERING TYPES

Modal fingerings can be the same as major scales, as long as you are mindful that the root is a different note. However, different fingering types are more or less commonly useful for the various modes, and some additional fingerings are also commonly used that are usually impractical for major (though still possible).

We will work with fingering types for some of the most common modes: Dorian, Mixolydian, and Aeolian. The fingering types are listed in order of usefulness. Some of the modal fingering types are identical (or nearly identical) to the fingering types of the major scale/Ionian mode.

Dorian

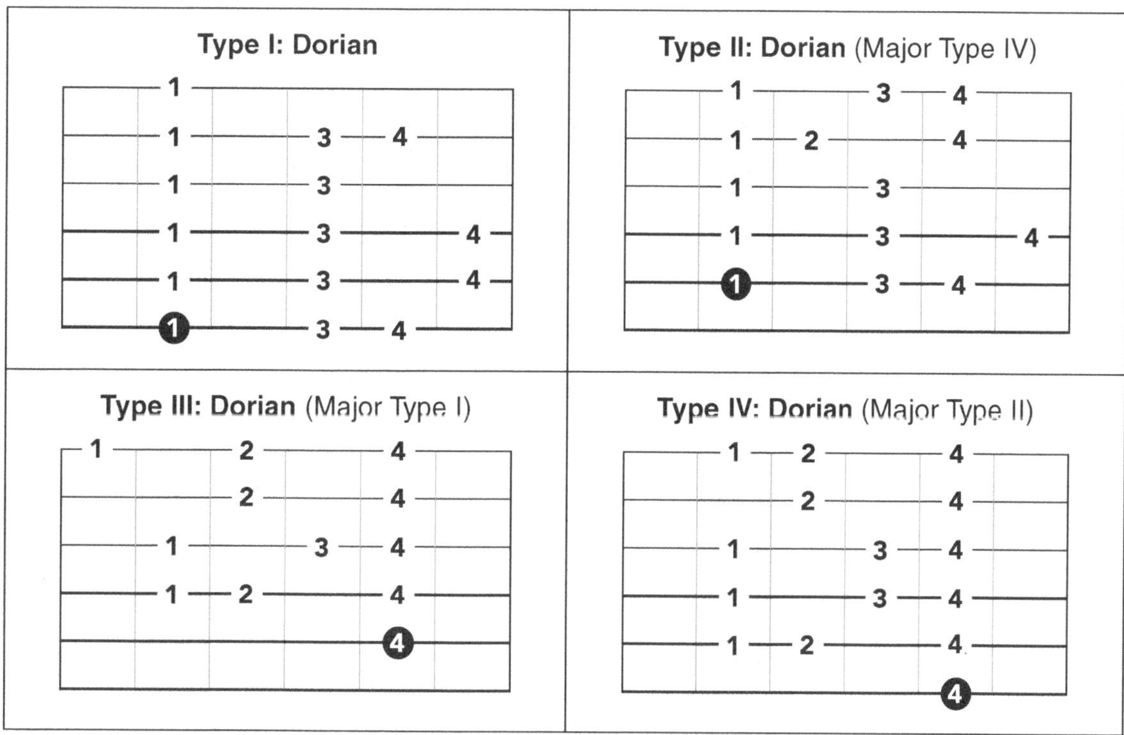

FIG. 5.2. Fingering Types for Dorian

Mixolydian

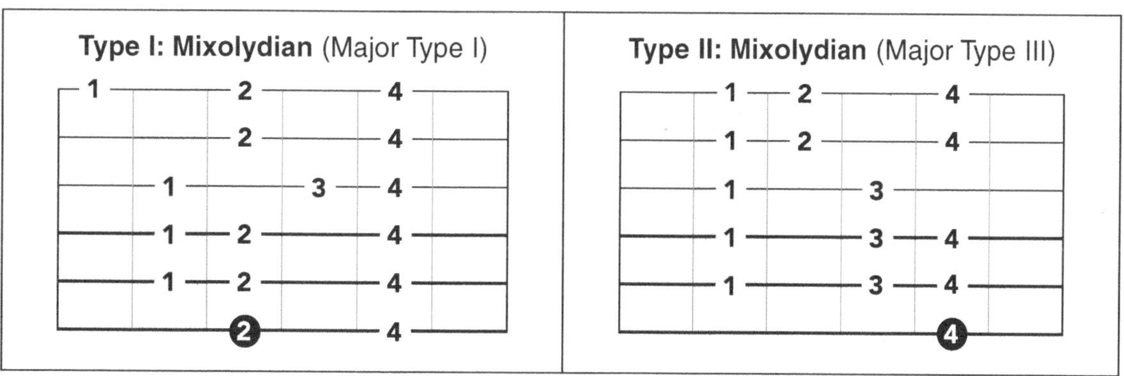

FIG. 5.3. Fingering Types for Mixolydian

Mode Practice

Use the major-scale range studies, position studies, and transposition charts for each of the modes.

ETUDES

Modal Vamps

FIG. 5.4. Modal Vamps

D Natural Minor Etude

FIG. 5.5. D Natural Minor Etude

CHAPTER 6

Harmonic Minor

W H W W H m3 H

Harmonic minor is like natural minor (or Aeolian) with a raised seventh degree. This scale can also be described as being like a major scale with a ♭3 and ♭6. Its notes are in the pattern: W H W W H m3 H.

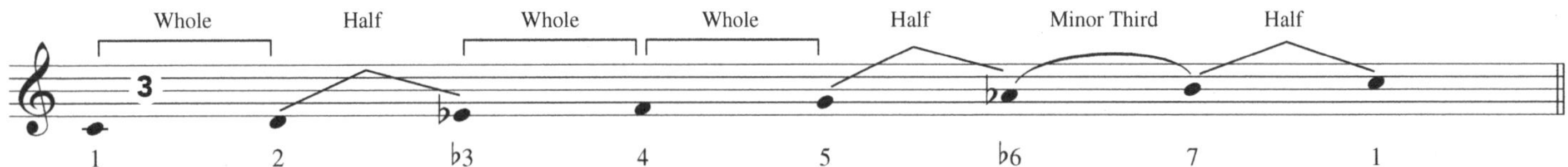

FIG. 6.1. C Harmonic Minor

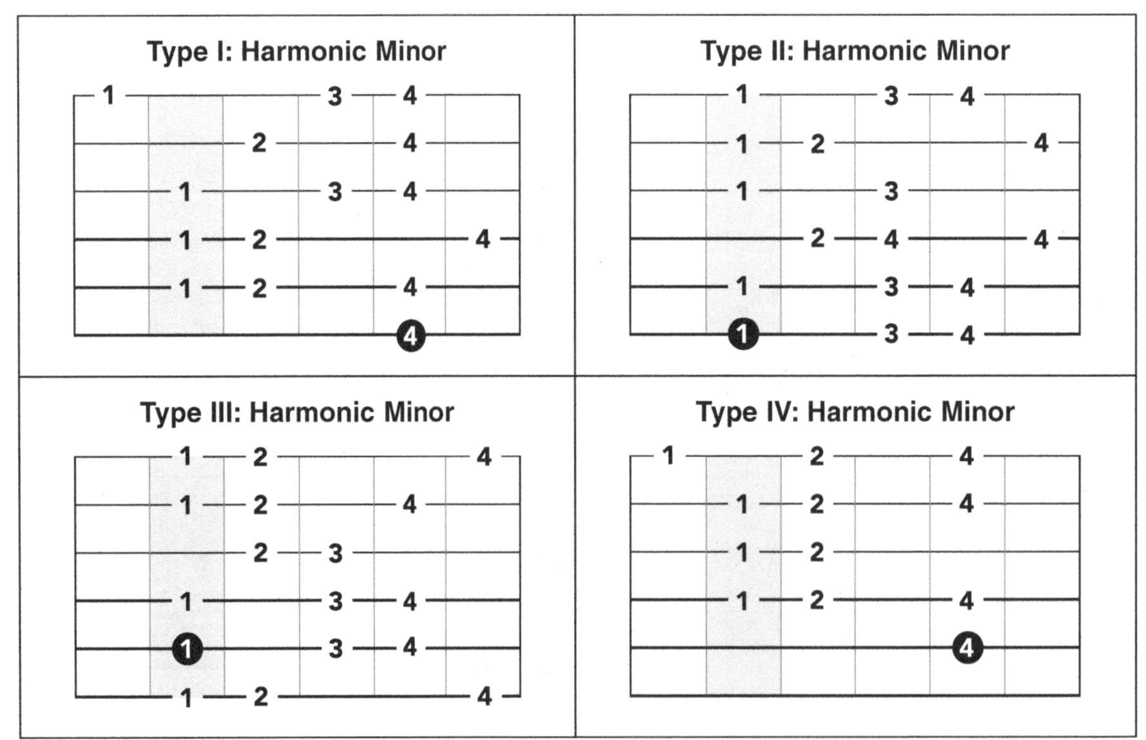

FIG. 6.2. Fingering Types for Harmonic Minor

HARMONIC MINORS		POSITIONS											
		1	2	3	4	5	6	7	8	9	10	11	12
FINGERING TYPES	I	A♭	A	B♭	B	C	C♯	D	E♭	E	F	F♯	G
	II	F	F♯	G	A♭	A	B♭	B	C	C♯	D	E♭	E
	III	B♭	B	C	C♯	D	E♭	E	F	F♯	G	A♭	A
	IV	C♯	D	E♭	E	F	F♯	G	A♭	A	B♭	B	C

FIG. 6.3. Harmonic Minor Fingering Types, Positions, and Tonics

RANGE STUDIES

FIG. 6.4. Harmonic Minor Range Studies

Three-Octave Scales: Harmonic Minor

FIG. 6.5. G Harmonic Minor in Three Octaves 1

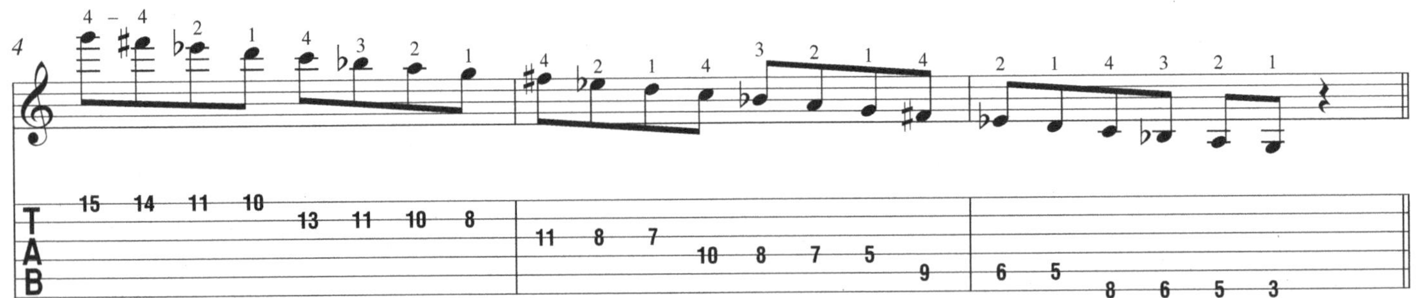

FIG. 6.6. G Harmonic Minor in Three Octaves 2

POSITION STUDIES

Type II: A Harmonic Minor
Root
Root

Type III: D Harmonic Minor
Root
Root

Type IV: F Harmonic Minor
Root
Root

Position 7

Type I: D Harmonic Minor
Root
Root

Type II: B Harmonic Minor
Root
Root

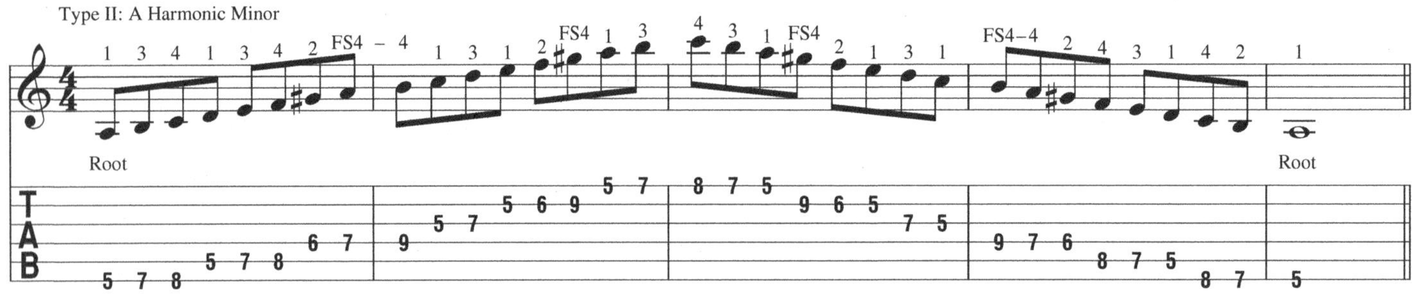

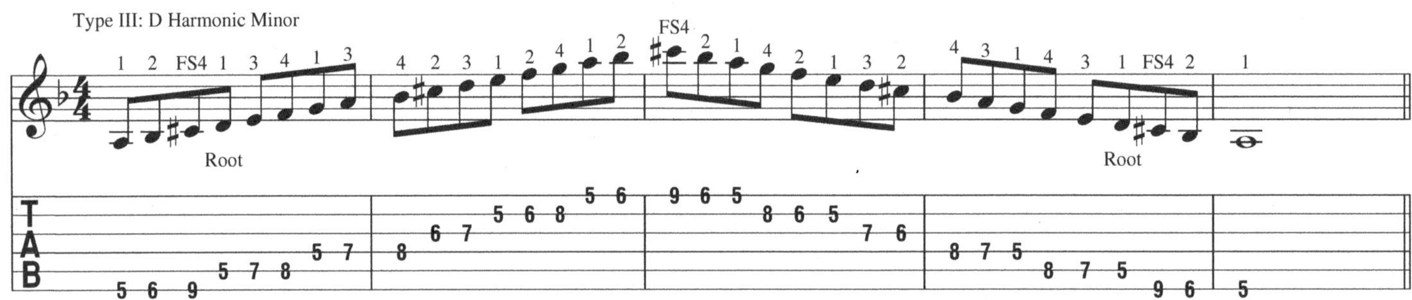

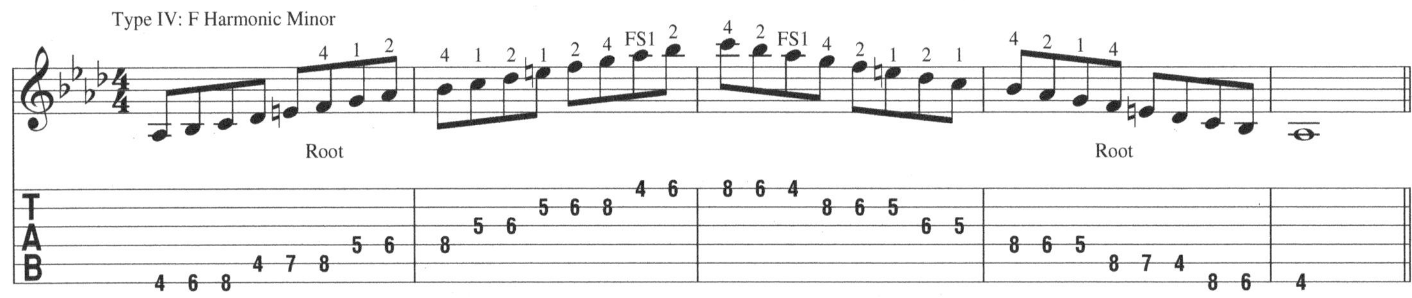

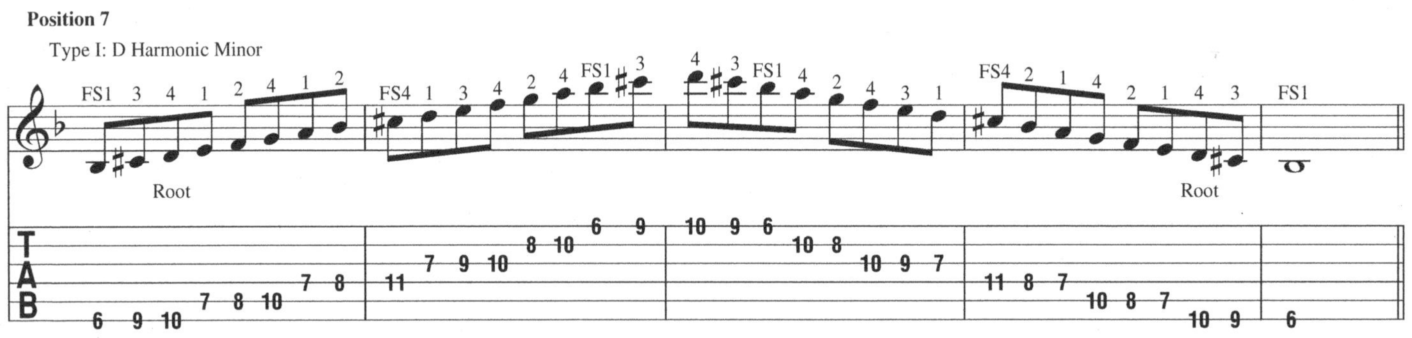

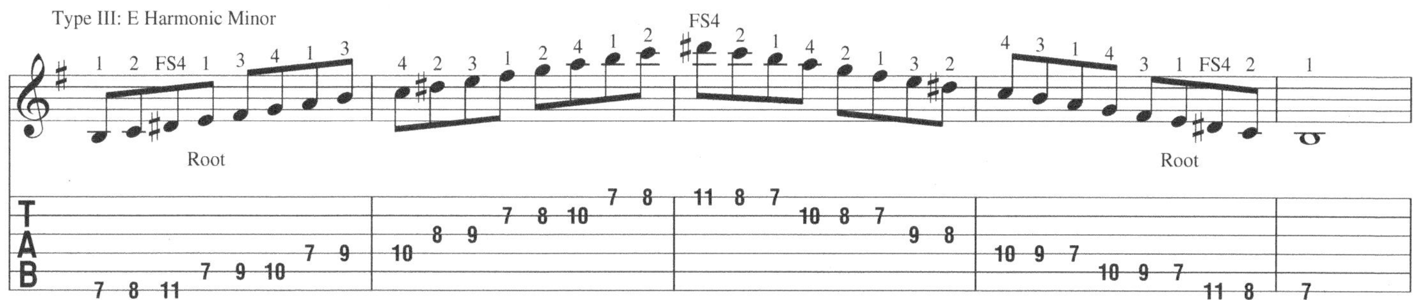

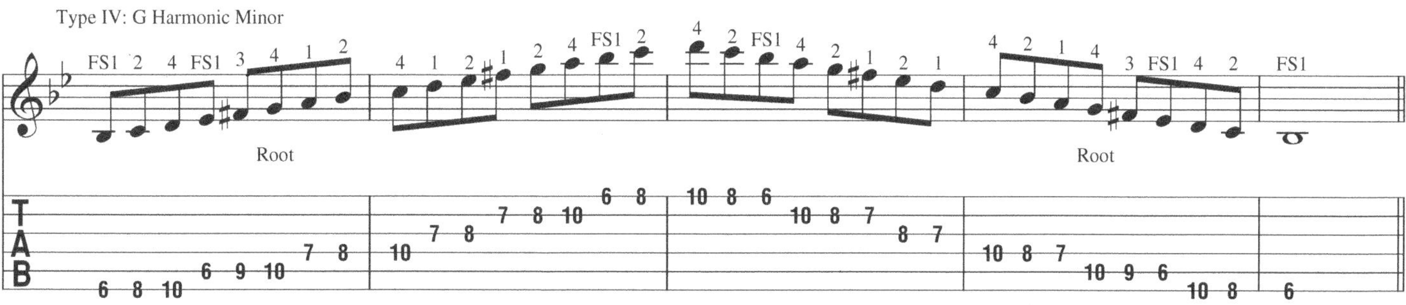

FIG. 6.7. Harmonic Minor Position Studies

MODES OF HARMONIC MINOR

Here are the modes of harmonic minor. The naming conventions for modes of harmonic minor are not universal, but these are the ones we use at Berklee.

FIG. 6.8. Modes of Harmonic Minor

TRANSPOSITIONS

FIG. 6.9. Transpositions of Harmonic Minor

ETUDES

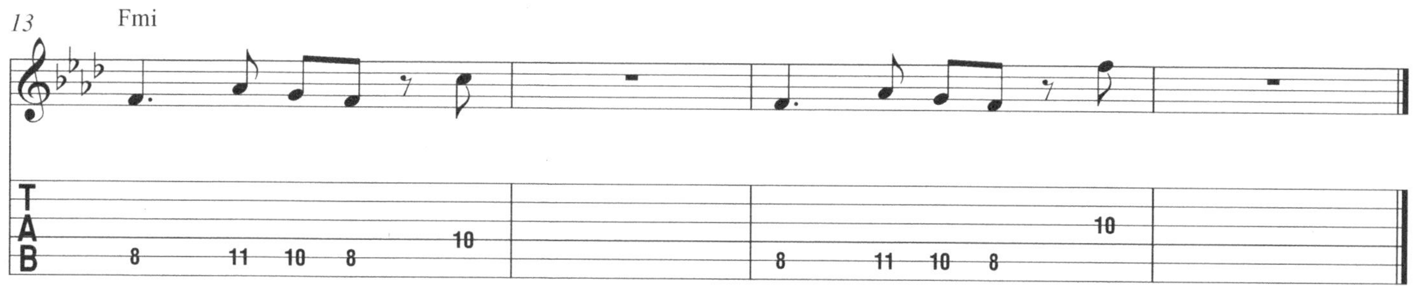

FIG. 6.10. Harmonic Minor Etude

Croatian Waltz

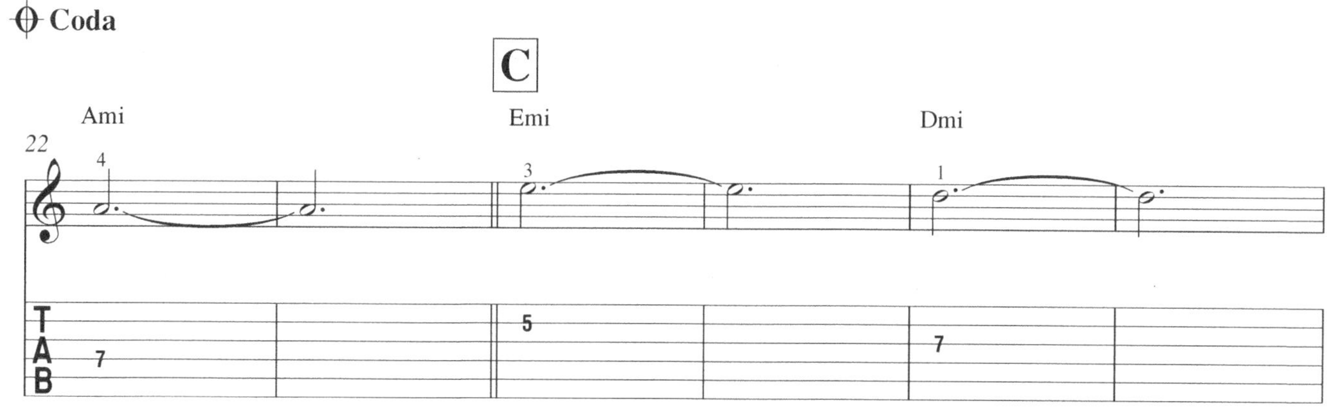

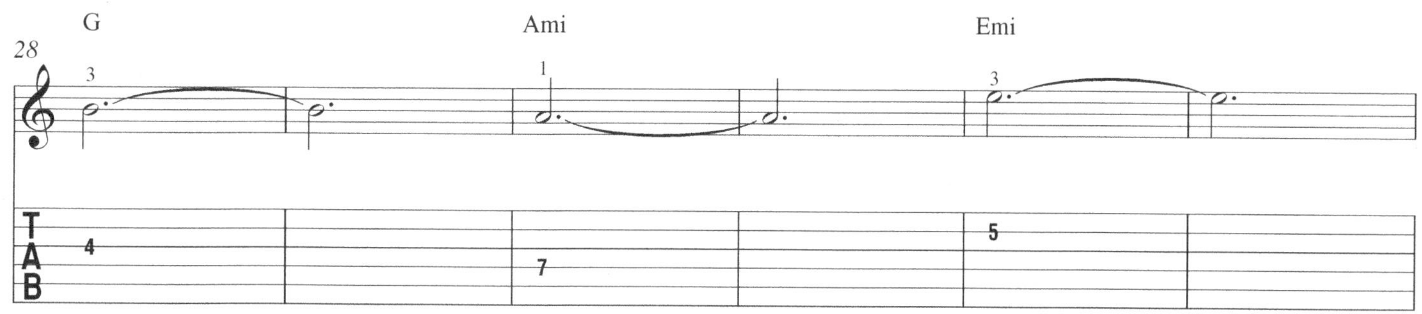

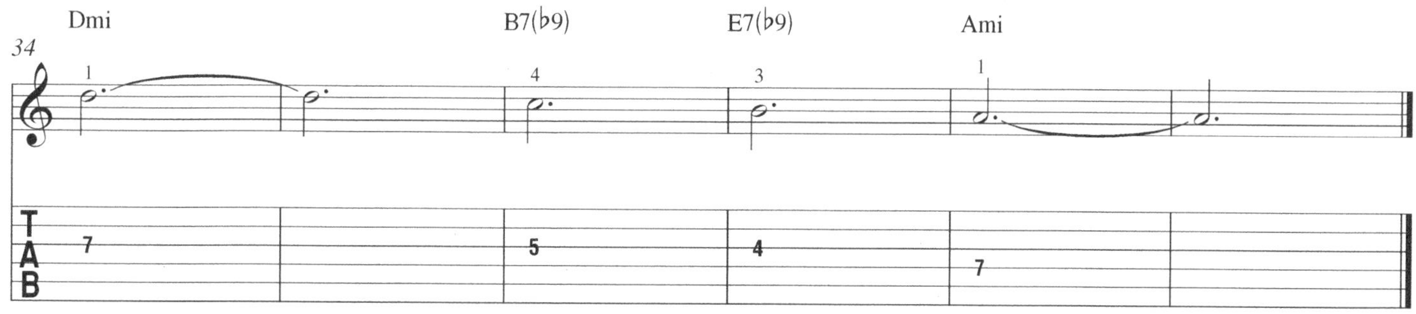

FIG. 6.11. Croatian Waltz (Harmonic Minor Etude)

CHAPTER 7

Melodic Minor

W H W W W W H

The melodic minor is only one note different than the major scale. It's the same scale, really, except that minor has a minor 3 instead of a major 3. Its notes are in the pattern: W H W W W W H.

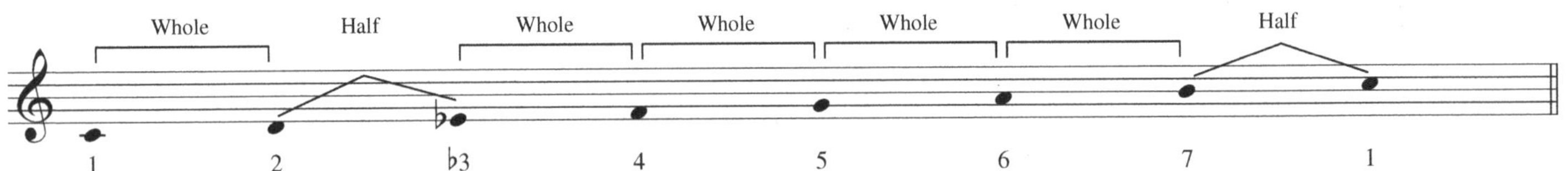

FIG. 7.1. C Melodic Minor Scale

"JAZZ" MELODIC MINOR

You may have been taught that the melodic minor has a raised 6 and 7 ascending and a lowered 6 and 7 descending. Traditionally, that is how the scale was used. However, it is more common in jazz and other improvised music to use the raised 6 and 7 both ascending and descending. For that reason, when the scale is played this way, it is often called a "jazz melodic minor." For our purposes, however, we'll just call it "melodic minor."

FINGERINGS

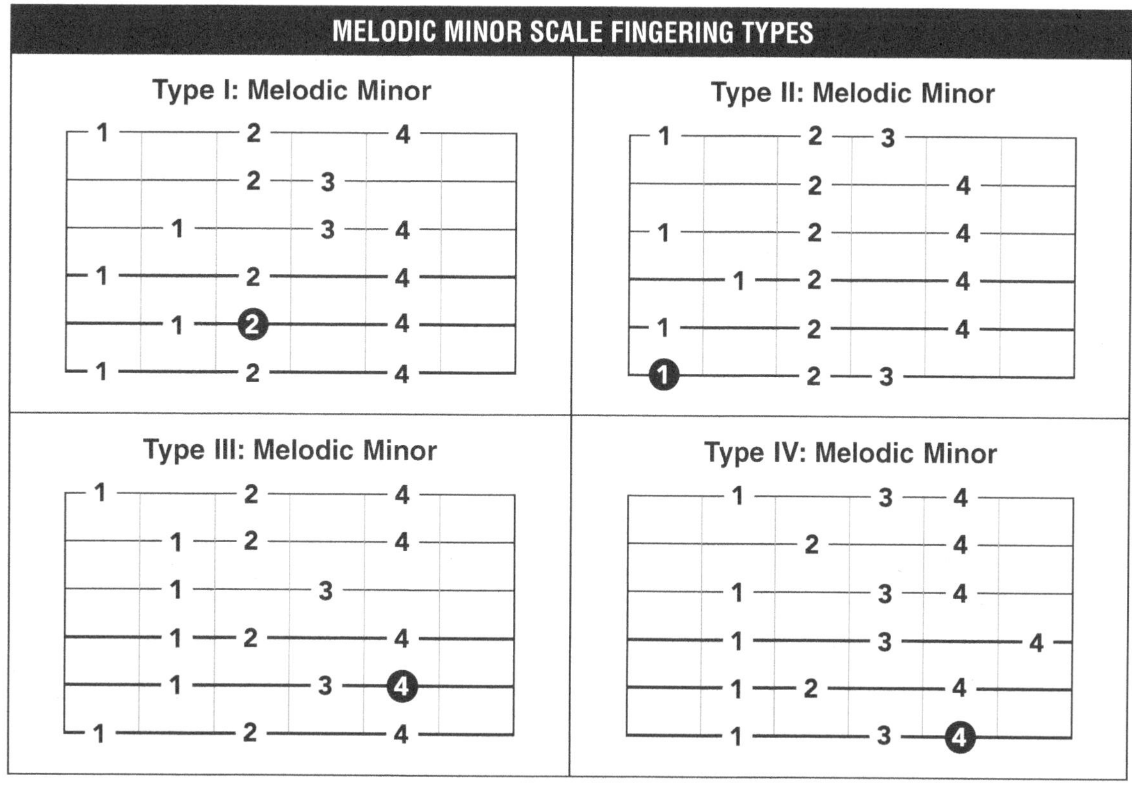

FIG. 7.2. Fingering Types for Melodic Minor

MELODIC MINOR		POSITIONS											
		1	2	3	4	5	6	7	8	9	10	11	12
FINGERING TYPES	I Two First-Finger Stretches	(B)	C	C♯	D	E♭	E	F	F♯	G	A♭	A	B♭
	II Four First-Finger Stretches	(E)	F	F♯	G	A♭	A	B♭	B	C	C♯	D	E♭
	III Two First-Finger Stretches	(C♯)	D	E♭	E	F	F♯	G	A♭	A	B♭	B	C
	IV One Fourth-Finger Stretch	A♭	A	B♭	B	C	C♯	D	E♭	E	F	F♯	G

FIG. 7.3. Harmonic Minor Fingering Types, Positions, and Tonics

RANGE STUDIES

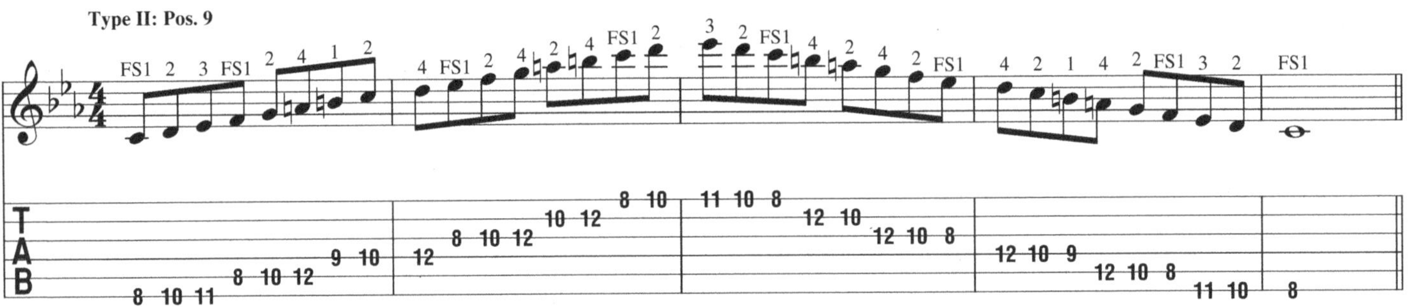

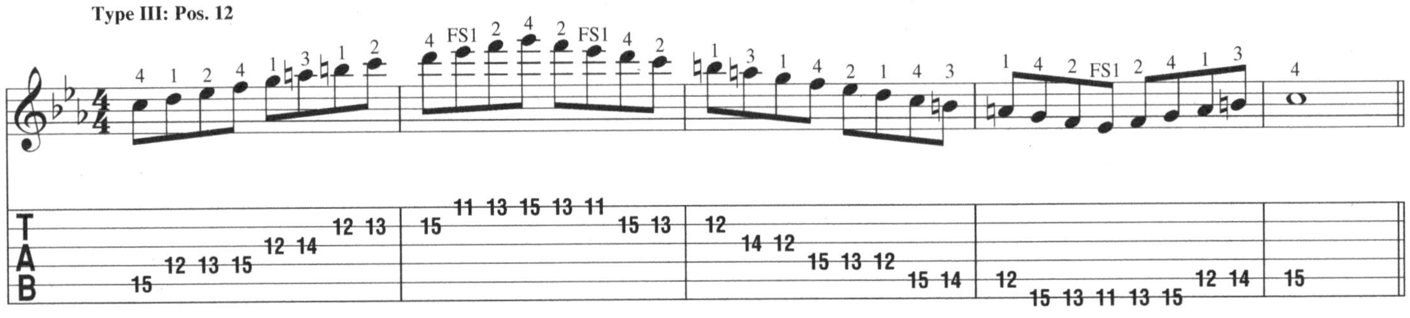

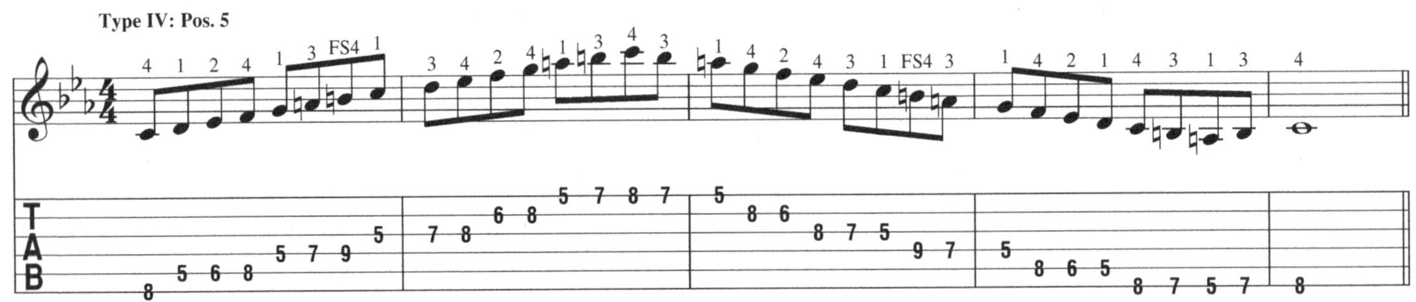

FIG. 7.4. Range Studies for C Melodic Minor

Three-Octave Scales: Melodic Minor

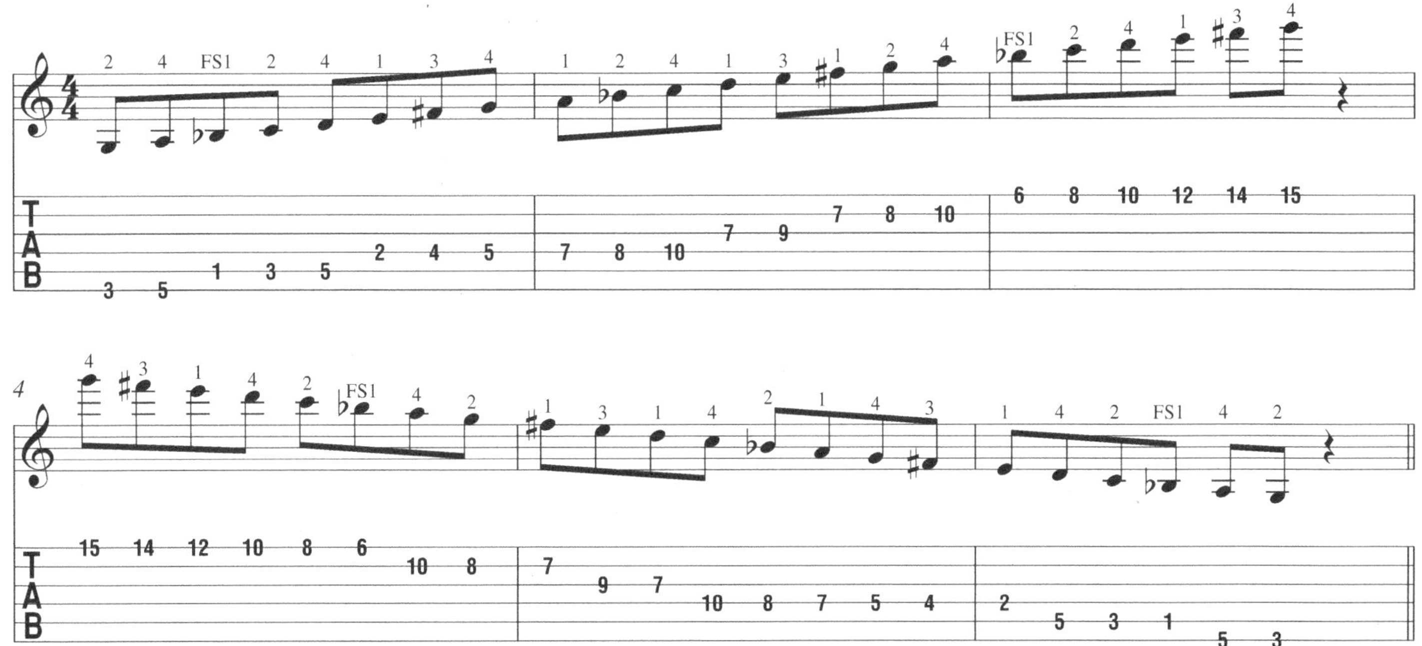

FIG. 7.5. G Melodic Minor Scale in Three Octaves 1

FIG. 7.6. G Melodic Minor Scale in Three Octaves 2

POSITION STUDIES

Position 2

Type I: C Melodic Minor

Type II: F Melodic Minor

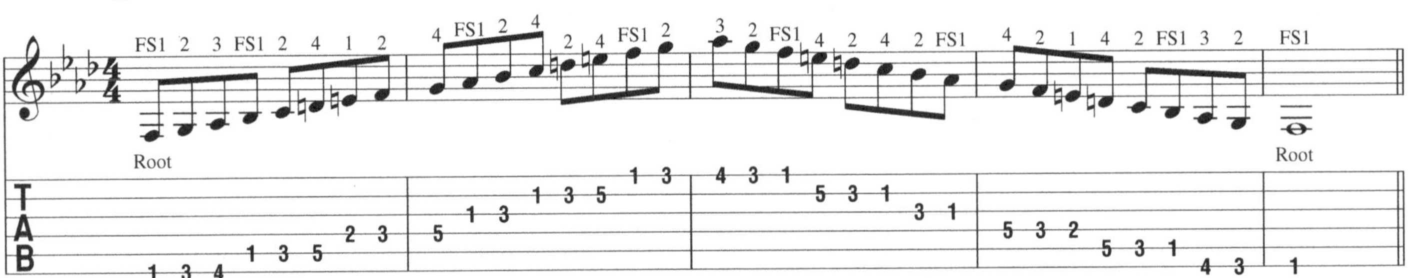

Type III: D Melodic Minor

Type IV: A Melodic Minor

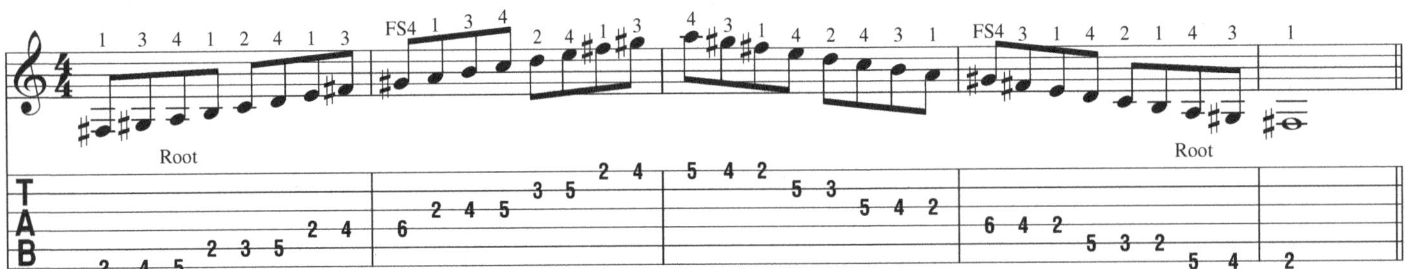

Position 5

Type I: E♭ Melodic Minor

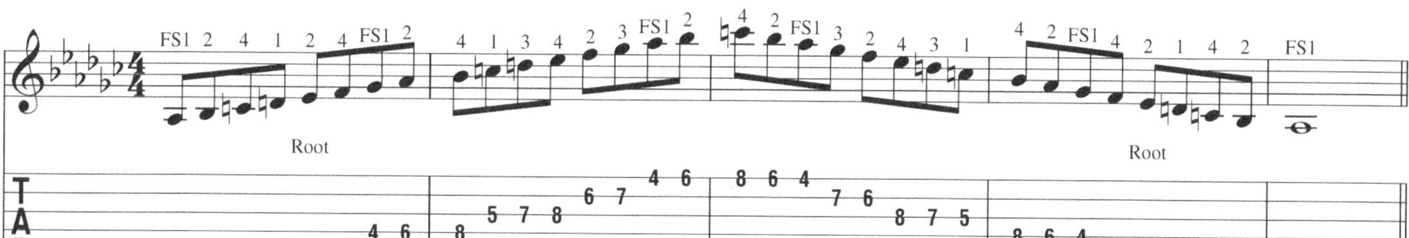

Type II: A♭ Melodic Minor

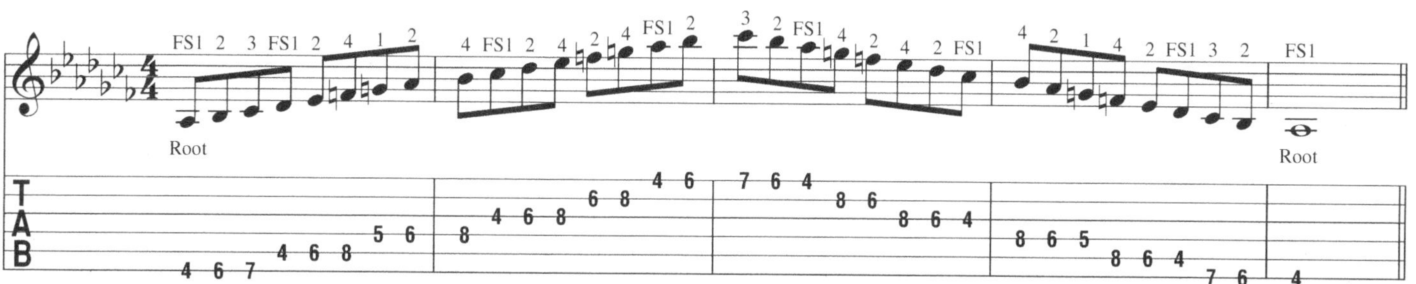

Type III: F Melodic Minor

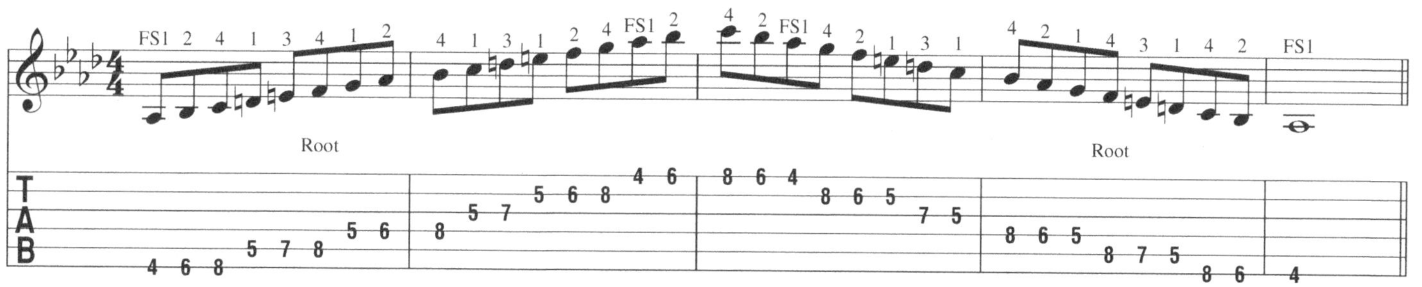

Type IV: C Melodic Minor

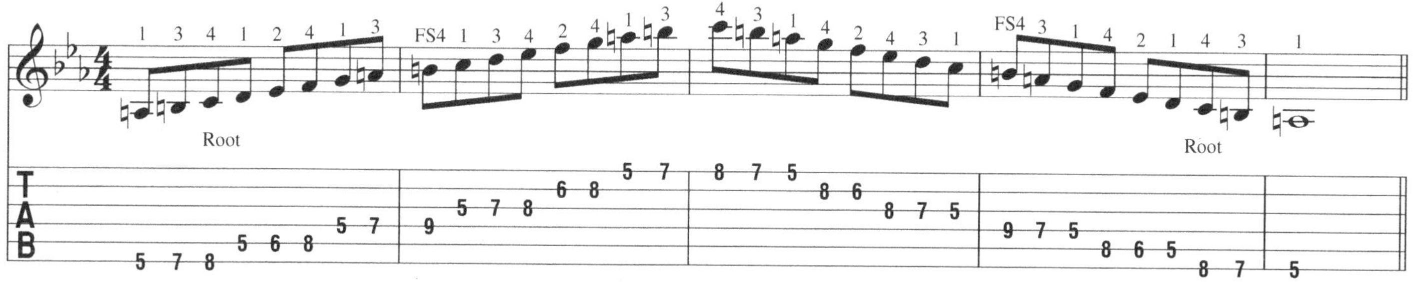

Position 7

Type I: F Melodic Minor

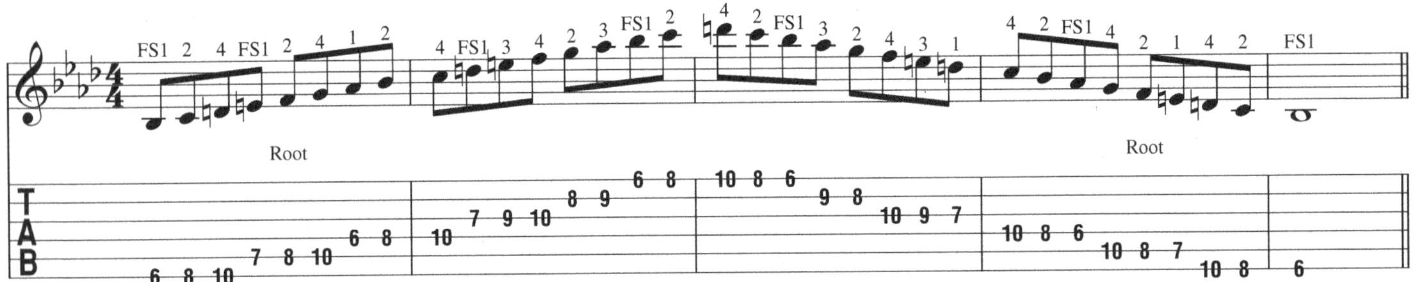

Type II: B♭ Melodic Minor

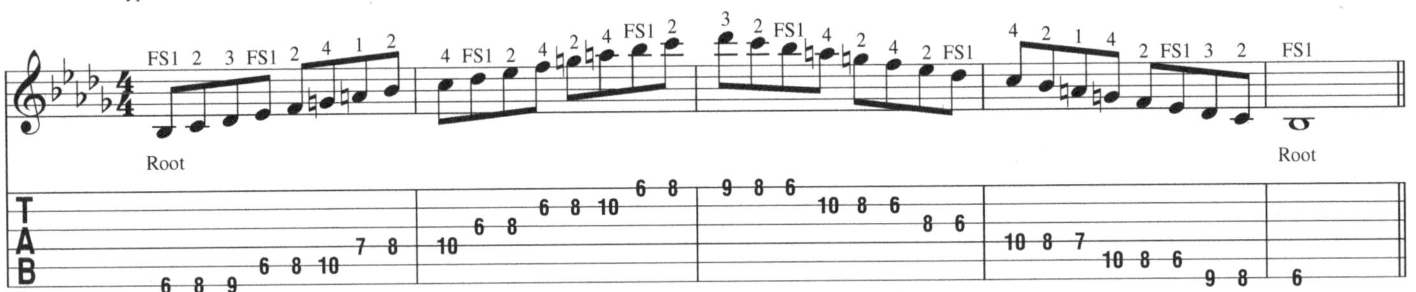

Type III: G Melodic Minor

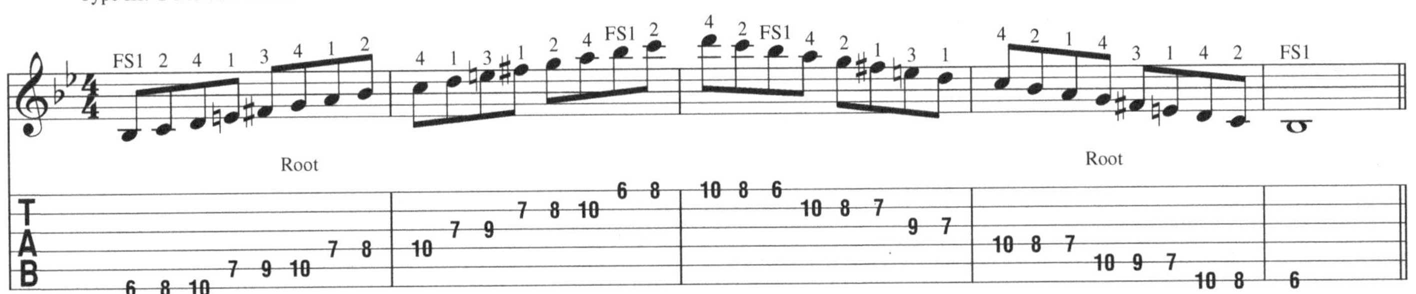

Type IV: D Melodic Minor

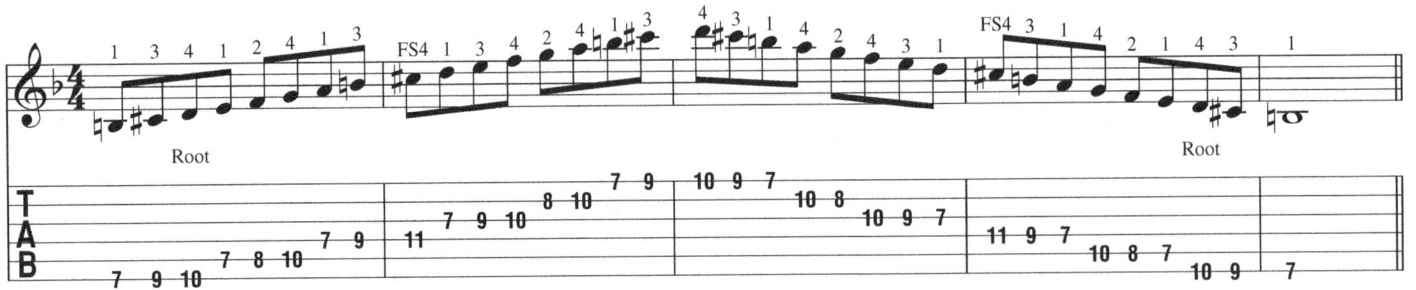

FIG. 7.7. Position Studies for Melodic Minor

MODES

FIG. 7.8. Modes of Melodic Minor

TRANSPOSITION

FIG. 7.9. Transpositions of Melodic Minor

ETUDE

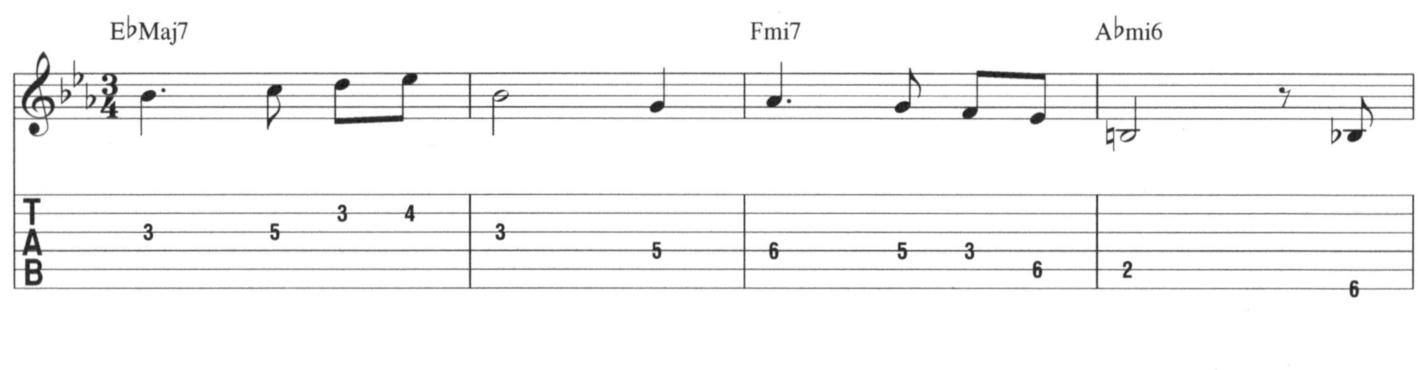

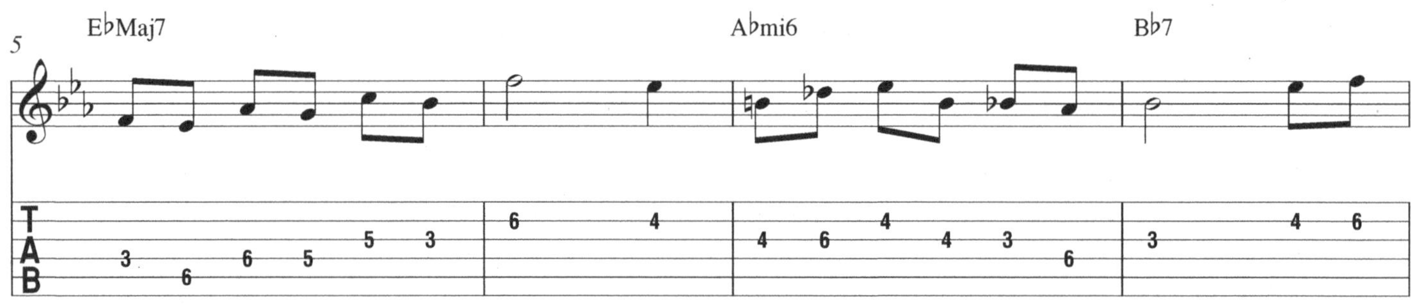

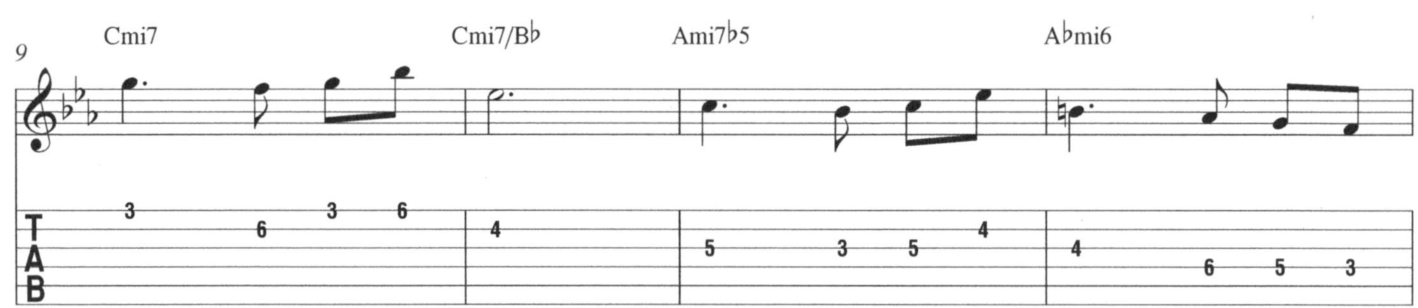

FIG. 7.10. Melodic Minor Etude

CHAPTER 8

Whole Tone

W W W W W W

The whole tone scale consists of six notes, all a whole step apart: W W W W W W. Since they are all the same interval apart, the scale is symmetrical. There is not relative tension between notes or different functionality, so each note has an equal sense of being the tonic. There are really only two whole tone scales.

FIG. 8.1. Whole Tone Scale

FINGERING

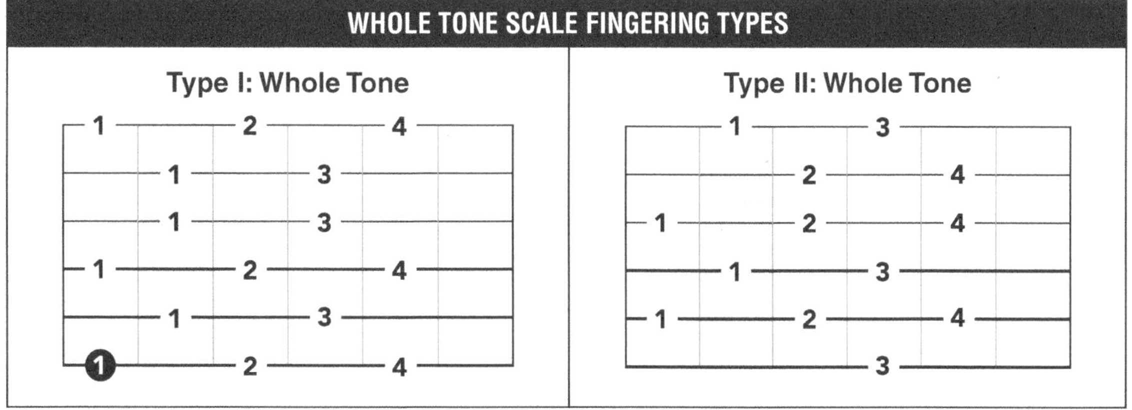

FIG. 8.2. Fingering Types for the Whole Tone Scale

WHOLE TONE		POSITIONS											
		1	2	3	4	5	6	7	8	9	10	11	12
FINGERING TYPES	I	E	F	F♯	G	A♭	A	B♭	B	C	C♯	D	E♭
	II	F	F♯	G	A♭	A	B♭	B	C	C♯	D	E♭	E

FIG. 8.3. Whole Tone Fingering Types, Positions, and Tonics

RANGE STUDIES

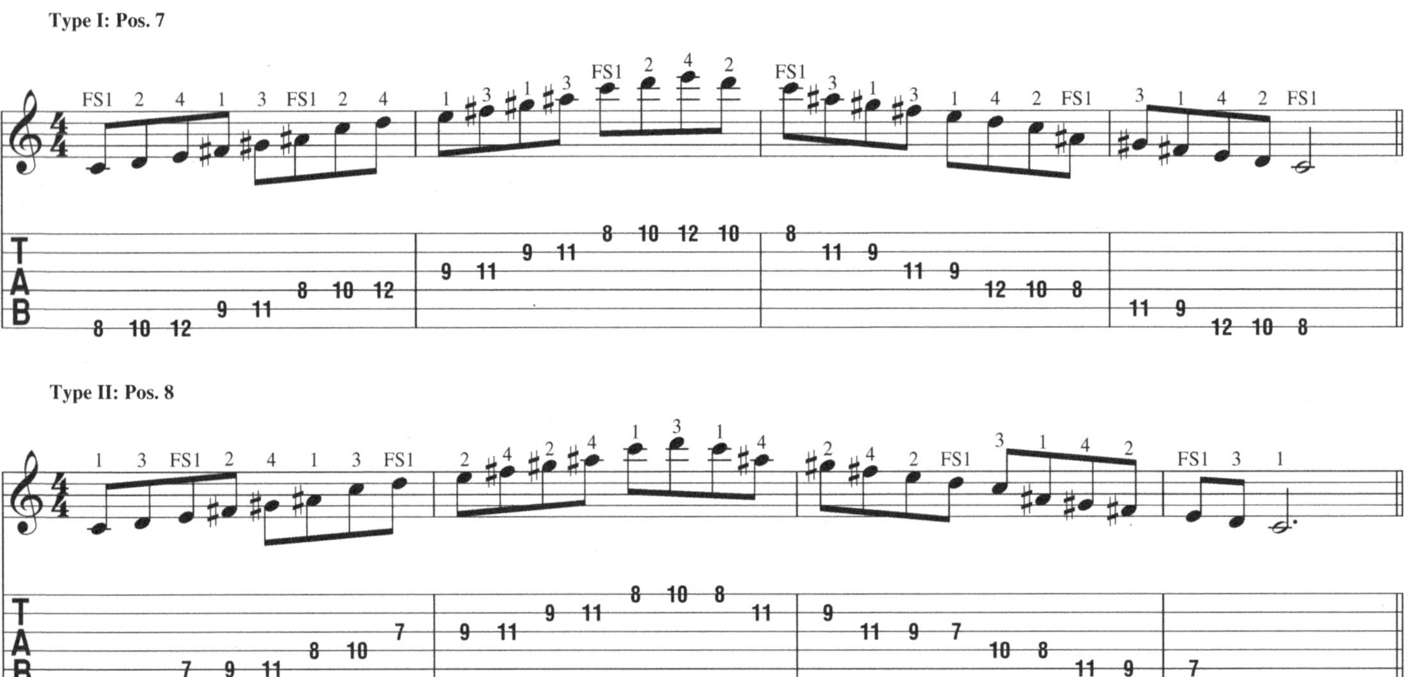

FIG. 8.4. Range Studies for Whole Tone Scale

Three-Octave Scales: Whole Tone

FIG. 8.5. G Whole Tone Scale in Three Octaves

POSITION STUDIES

FIG. 8.6. Position Studies for Whole Tone Scale

ETUDE

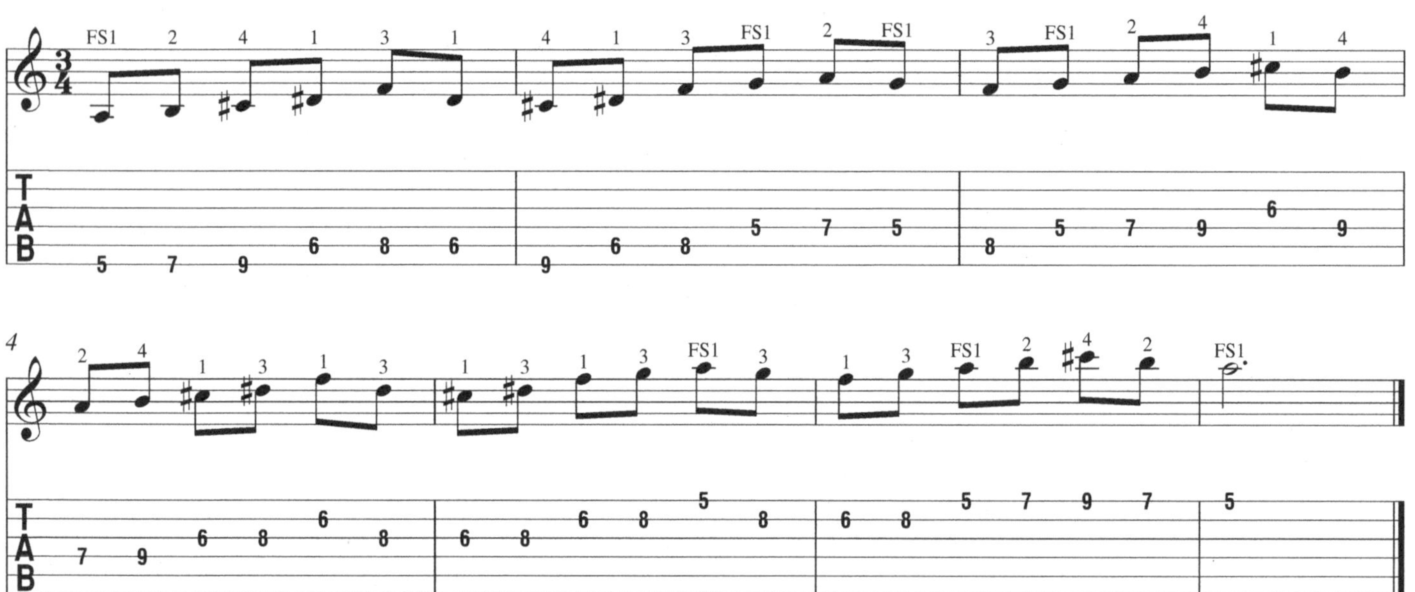

FIG. 8.7. Whole Tone Etude

CHAPTER 9

Diminished

W H W H W H W H

The diminished scale is an octatonic (eight-note) scale consisting of alternating whole steps and half steps: W H W H W H W H. Every other note outlines the chord tones of a diminished seventh chord.

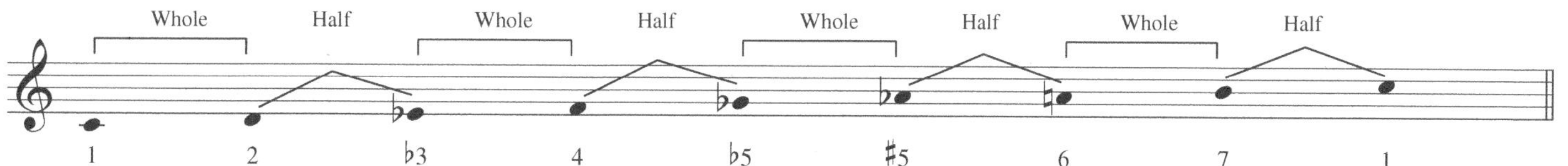

FIG. 9.1. C Diminished Scale

FINGERING

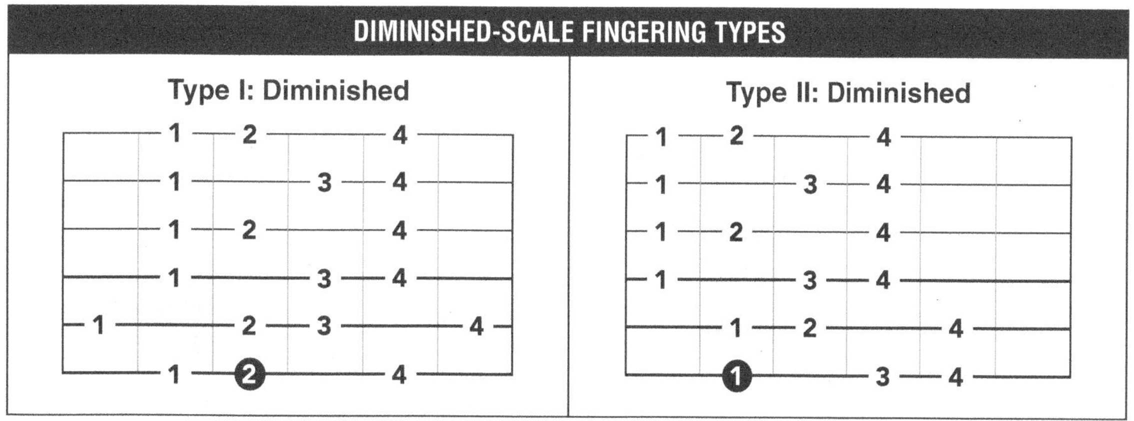

FIG. 9.2. Fingering Types for Diminished

DIMINISHED		POSITIONS											
		1	2	3	4	5	6	7	8	9	10	11	12
FINGERING TYPES	I	F♯	G	A♭	A	B♭	B	C	C♯	D	E♭	E	F
	II	F	F♯	G	A♭	A	B♭	B	C	C♯	D	E♭	E

FIG. 9.3. Diminished-Scale Fingering Types, Positions, and Tonics

RANGE STUDIES

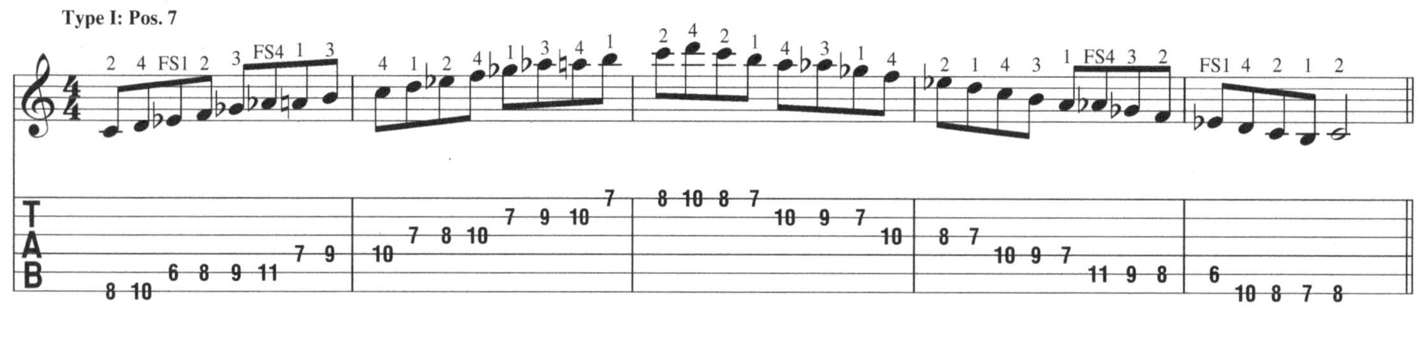

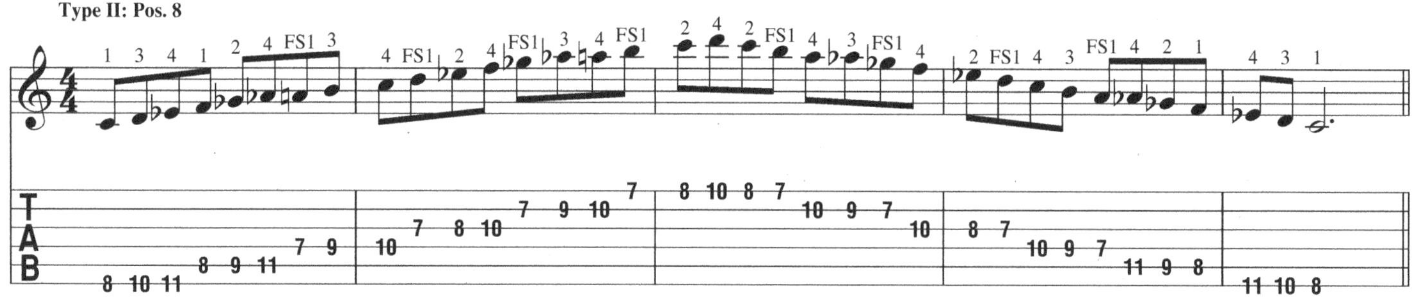

FIG. 9.4. Range Studies for C Diminished Scale

Three Octave Scales: Diminished

FIG. 9.5. G Diminished Scale in Three Octaves

POSITION STUDIES

FIG. 9.6. Position Studies for Diminished Scales

TRANSPOSITION AND MODE (SYMMETRIC DIMINISHED)

The diminished scale is another symmetrical scale, with a regularly repeating pattern. It has three transpositions before the notes repeat in different modes.

FIG. 9.7. Transpositions of C Diminished

The mode of the diminished scale starts on the 2, resulting in a half-step/whole-step pattern, rather than the original whole-step/half-step pattern. This is called the *symmetric diminished scale*, or the *half-whole symmetric scale.*

H W H W H W H W

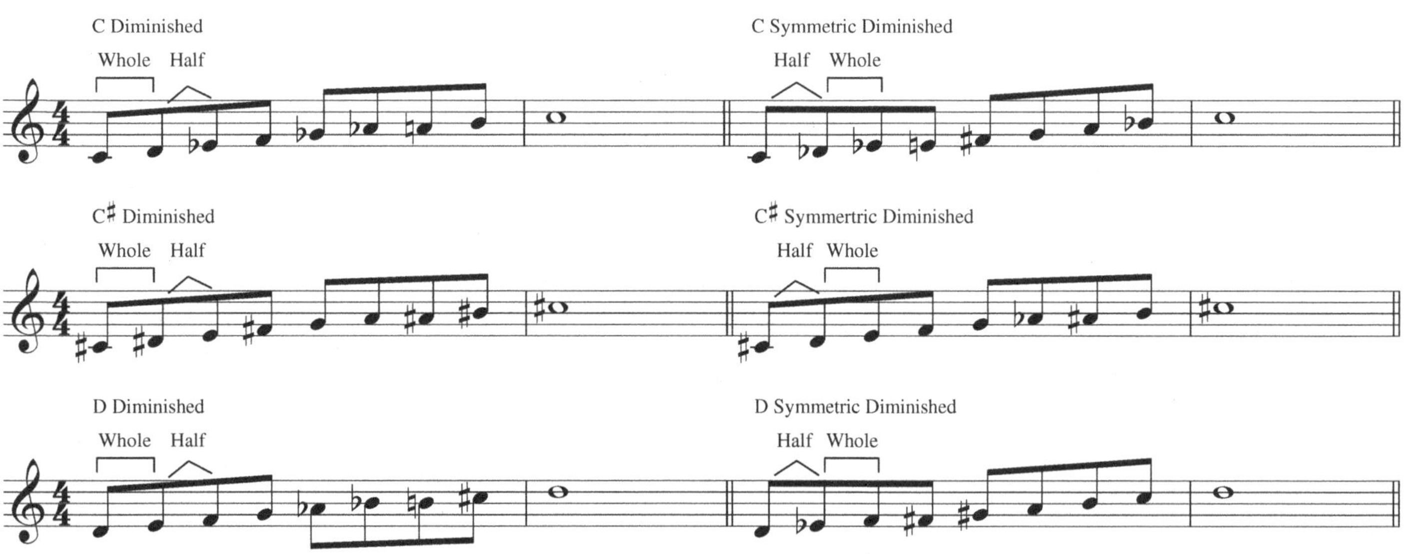

FIG. 9.8. Symmetric Diminished: The Mode of Diminished

Three-Octave Scales: Symmetric Diminished

FIG. 9.9. G Symmetric Diminished Scale in Three Octaves

ETUDE

FIG. 9.10. Symmetric Diminished Etude (On Dominant Seventh Chords)

CHAPTER 10

Chromatic

H H H H H H H H H H H H

The chromatic scale includes all twelve pitches of the octave, each a semitone apart: H H H H H H H H H H H H.

FIG. 10.1. C Chromatic Scale

FINGERING

Use type I (1st finger stretch) for ascending and type II (4th finger stretch) for descending.

CHROMATIC SCALE FINGERING TYPES	
Type I: Chromatic	**Type II: Chromatic**
1 — 1 — 2 — 3 — 4	1 — 2 — 3 — 4
1 — 2 — 3 — 4	1 — 2 — 3 — 4 — 4
1 — 1 — 2 — 3 — 4	1 — 2 — 3 — 4
1 — 1 — 2 — 3 — 4	1 — 2 — 3 — 4 — 4
1 — 1 — 2 — 3 — 4	1 — 2 — 3 — 4 — 4
❶ — 2 — 3 — 4	❶ — 2 — 3 — 4 — 4

FIG. 10.2. Chromatic Fingering Types

Since the chromatic scale is symmetrical, and any note can be a root, the chart in this case indicates that the type II fingerings are used for descending passages, starting on the fourth fret (minor third) above any position.

CHROMATIC		POSITIONS											
		1	2	3	4	5	6	7	8	9	10	11	12
FINGERING TYPES	I	F	F♯	G	A♭	A	B♭	B	C	C♯	D	E♭	E
	II	A♭	A	B♭	B	C	C♯	D	E♭	E	F	F♯	G

FIG. 10.3. Chromatic Fingering Types, Positions, and Tonics

RANGE STUDY

Type I: Pos. 8

Type II: Pos. 8

FIG. 10.4. Range Study for the C Chromatic Scale

Three-Octave Scales: Chromatic

FIG. 10.5. F Chromatic Scale in Three Octaves

POSITION STUDIES

Position 2

Type I: F♯ Chromatic

Type II: A Chromatic

Position 5

Type I: A Chromatic

Type II: C Chromatic

Type II: D Chromatic

FIG. 10.6. Position Studies for the C Chromatic Scale

ETUDE

7th Position

FIG. 10.7. Chromatic Scale Etude in 7th Position

CHAPTER 11

Intervallic Scale Practice

The following exercises show that scales can be practiced in intervals, rather than in simple sequential ascending or descending form. Here, examples are given of major scales in comfortable positions. Use this approach to practice a variety of scales, positions, and fingering types.

Thirds

FIG. 11.1. G Major in Thirds

Fourths

FIG. 11.2. G Major in Fourths

Fifths

FIG. 11.3. C Major in Fifths

Sixths

FIG. 11.4. B♭ Major in Sixths

Sevenths

FIG. 11.5. C Major in Sevenths

AFTERWORD

Mastering any instrument involves practice, and practice involves repetition. I suggest going back periodically through this book and reviewing both what you found easy (maybe playing the scales and exercises at a variety of tempos) and what you found hard (playing slowly and noticing where you have some problems and seeing your improvement).

Good luck with your music and your performing.

—Larry Baione

APPENDIX

Chord-Scale Relationships

CHORD	SCALES
Major 7	• Major (Ionian) • Lydian
Major 6	• Major (Ionian) • Lydian
Dominant 7	See figure A.2.
Minor 7	• Dorian • Major Scale from Chord 3, 6, or 7 • Aeolian • Phrygian
Minor 6	Melodic Minor
Minor 7♭5	Major scale a half step above the chord root
Diminished 7	• Whole/Half Diminished from any chord tone. • Treat as Dominant 7(♭9). • ♯I°7 can be treated as VI7(♭9). C°7 in key of C can be treated as B7(♭9). • II°7 can be treated at II7(♭9). D°7 in key of C can be treated as E7(♭9). See figure A.2.
Augmented	Whole tone
Minor Major 7	• Melodic minor • Harmonic minor

FIG. A.1. Chord and Scale Pairings

Chord-Scale Relationships on a Dominant 7 Chord

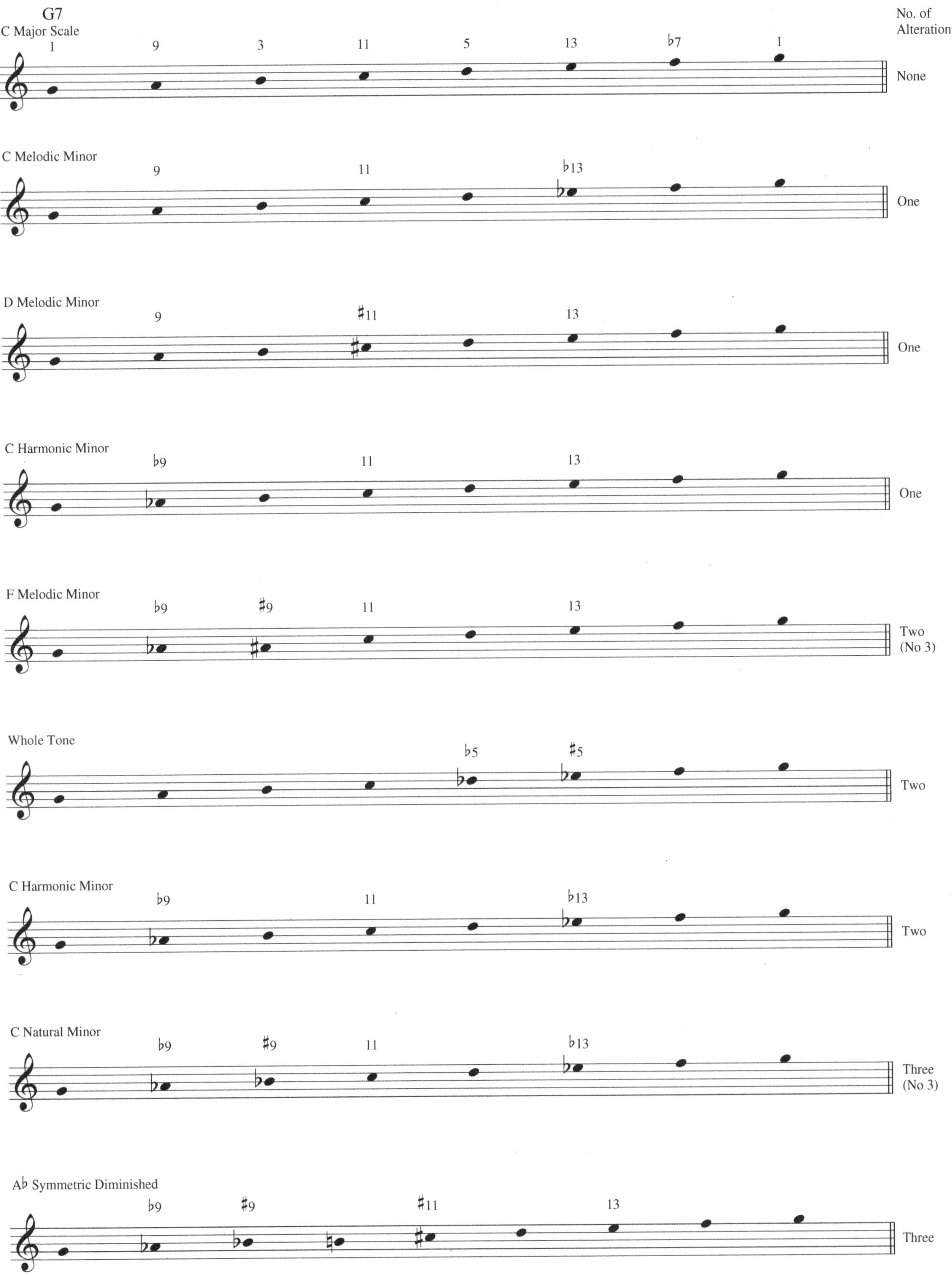

FIG. A.2. Dominant 7 Chord Scales

ABOUT THE AUTHOR

(Photo by Kim Perlak)

Larry Baione has been chair of the Berklee College of Music Guitar Department since 1990 and a Berklee faculty member since 1974. He has studied with William Leavitt, Lenzy Wallace, Mick Goodrick, Bill Harris, Bucky Pizzarelli, and Jim Hall. He received a bachelors in music from Berklee and a masters in music from New England Conservatory. When attending Berklee, he received the Downbeat Hall of Fame Scholarship award.

After graduating Berklee, Larry was principal guitarist in the U.S. Army Band, stationed in Washington, D.C. He performed in the White House and throughout the United States with the Army Band. In 1996, Baione toured South America for the U.S. Department of State as one of the inaugural Jazz Ambassadors representing the unique American art form.

Larry is the author of *Berklee Practice Method: Guitar.* He produced fourteen hours of video to accompany *A Modern Method for Guitar, Volume 1* (by William Leavitt), and he has produced numerous courses for Berklee Online, including *Guitar Scales 101.* He continues to perform and give clinics throughout the world in jazz, concert, and recording ensembles, in settings that range from solo guitar to big band. Larry's recent recording *Playing Time* consists of original compositions and standards in a trio setting.

More Fine Publications

GUITAR

BERKLEE ESSENTIAL GUITAR SONGBOOK
Kim Perlak, Sheryl Bailey, and Members of the Berklee Guitar Department Faculty
00350814 Book.......$22.99

BERKLEE GUITAR CHORD DICTIONARY
Rick Peckham
50449546 Jazz – Book.......$14.99
50449596 Rock – Book.......$12.99

BERKLEE GUITAR STYLE STUDIES
Jim Kelly
00200377 Book/Online Media.......$24.99

BERKLEE GUITAR THEORY
Kim Perlak and Members of the Berklee Guitar Department Faculty
00276326 Book.......$24.99

BLUES GUITAR TECHNIQUE
Michael Williams
50449623 Book/Online Audio.......$29.99

CLASSICAL TECHNIQUE FOR THE MODERN GUITARIST
Kim Perlak
00148781 Book/Online Audio.......$19.99

COUNTRY GUITAR STYLES
Mike Ihde
00254157 Book/Online Audio.......$24.99

CREATIVE CHORDAL HARMONY FOR GUITAR
Mick Goodrick and Tim Miller
50449613 Book/Online Audio.......$22.99

FUNK/R&B GUITAR
Thaddeus Hogarth
50449569 Book/Online Audio.......$19.99

GUITAR SWEEP PICKING
Joe Stump
00151223 Book/Online Audio.......$19.99

JAZZ GUITAR FRETBOARD NAVIGATION
Mark White
00154107 Book/Online Audio.......$22.99

MODAL VOICINGS FOR GUITAR
Rick Peckham
00151227 Book/Online Media.......$24.99

A MODERN METHOD FOR GUITAR – VOLUMES 1-3 COMPLETE*
William Leavitt
00292990 Book/Online Media.......$49.99
**Individual volumes, media options, and supporting songbooks available.*

A MODERN METHOD FOR GUITAR SCALES
Larry Baione
00199318 Book.......$14.99

TRIADS FOR THE IMPROVISING GUITARIST
Jane Miller
00284857 Book/Online Audio.......$22.99

Berklee Press publications feature material developed at Berklee College of Music.
To browse the complete Berklee Press Catalog, go to
www.berkleepress.com

BASS

BERKLEE JAZZ BASS
Rich Appleman, Whit Browne & Bruce Gertz
50449636 Book/Online Audio.......$22.99

CHORD STUDIES FOR ELECTRIC BASS
Rich Appleman & Joseph Viola
50449750 Book.......$17.99

FINGERSTYLE FUNK BASS LINES
Joe Santerre
50449542 Book/Online Audio.......$24.99

FUNK BASS FILLS
Anthony Vitti
50449608 Book/Online Audio.......$22.99

INSTANT BASS
Danny Morris
50449502 Book/CD.......$9.99

METAL BASS LINES
David Marvuglio
00122465 Book/Online Audio.......$19.99

READING CONTEMPORARY ELECTRIC BASS
Rich Appleman
50449770 Book.......$22.99

PIANO/KEYBOARD

BERKLEE JAZZ KEYBOARD HARMONY
Suzanna Sifter
00138874 Book/Online Audio.......$29.99

BERKLEE JAZZ PIANO
Ray Santisi
50448047 Book/Online Audio.......$22.99

BERKLEE JAZZ STANDARDS FOR SOLO PIANO
Robert Christopherson, Hey Rim Jeon, Ross Ramsay, Tim Ray
00160482 Book/Online Audio.......$22.99

CHORD-SCALE IMPROVISATION FOR KEYBOARD
Ross Ramsay
50449597 Book/CD.......$19.99

CONTEMPORARY PIANO TECHNIQUE
Stephany Tiernan
50449545 Book/DVD.......$39.99

HAMMOND ORGAN COMPLETE
Dave Limina
00237801 Book/Online Audio.......$24.99

JAZZ PIANO COMPING
Suzanne Davis
50449614 Book/Online Audio.......$22.99

LATIN JAZZ PIANO IMPROVISATION
Rebecca Cline
50449649 Book/Online Audio.......$29.99

PIANO ESSENTIALS
Ross Ramsay
50448046 Book/Online Audio.......$26.99

SOLO JAZZ PIANO
Neil Olmstead
50449641 Book/Online Audio.......$42.99

DRUMS

BEGINNING DJEMBE
Michael Markus & Joe Galeota
00148210 Book/Online Video.......$16.99

BERKLEE JAZZ DRUMS
Casey Scheuerell
50449612 Book/Online Audio.......$26.99

DRUM SET WARM-UPS
Rod Morgenstein
50449465 Book.......$15.99

A MANUAL FOR THE MODERN DRUMMER
Alan Dawson & Don DeMichael
50449560 Book.......$14.99

MASTERING THE ART OF BRUSHES
Jon Hazilla
50449459 Book/Online Audio.......$19.99

PHRASING
Russ Gold
00120209 Book/Online Media.......$19.99

WORLD JAZZ DRUMMING
Mark Walker
50449568 Book/CD.......$27.99

BERKLEE PRACTICE METHOD

GET YOUR BAND TOGETHER
With additional volumes for other instruments, plus a teacher's guide.

Bass
Rich Appleman, John Repucci and the Berklee Faculty
50449427 Book/CD.......$24.99

Drum Set
Ron Savage, Casey Scheuerell and the Berklee Faculty
50449429 Book/CD.......$17.99

Guitar
Larry Baione and the Berklee Faculty
50449426 Book/CD.......$19.99

Keyboard
Russell Hoffmann, Paul Schmeling and the Berklee Faculty
50449428 Book/Online Audio.......$19.99

VOICE

BELTING
Jeannie Gagné
00124984 Book/Online Media.......$22.99

THE CONTEMPORARY SINGER
Anne Peckham
50449595 Book/Online Audio.......$29.99

JAZZ VOCAL IMPROVISATION
Mili Bermejo
00159290 Book/Online Audio.......$19.99

TIPS FOR SINGERS
Carolyn Wilkins
50449557 Book/CD.......$19.95

VOCAL WORKOUTS FOR THE CONTEMPORARY SINGER
Anne Peckham
50448044 Book/Online Audio.......$27.99

YOUR SINGING VOICE
Jeannie Gagné
50449619 Book/Online Audio.......$29.99

WOODWINDS & BRASS

TRUMPET SOUND EFFECTS
Craig Pederson & Ueli Dörig
00121626 Book/Online Audio............$14.99

SAXOPHONE SOUND EFFECTS
Ueli Dörig
50449628 Book/Online Audio..........$17.99

THE TECHNIQUE OF THE FLUTE
Joseph Viola
00214012 Book......................................$19.99

STRINGS/ROOTS MUSIC

BERKLEE HARP
Felice Pomeranz
00144263 Book/Online Audio..........$24.99

BEYOND BLUEGRASS BANJO
Dave Hollander and Matt Glaser
50449610 Book/CD..............................$19.99

BEYOND BLUEGRASS MANDOLIN
John McGann and Matt Glaser
50449609 Book/CD..............................$19.99

BLUEGRASS FIDDLE & BEYOND
Matt Glaser
50449602 Book/CD..............................$19.99

CONTEMPORARY CELLO ETUDES
Mike Block
00159292 Book/Online Audio..........$24.99

EXPLORING CLASSICAL MANDOLIN
August Watters
00125040 Book/Online Media..........$24.99

THE IRISH CELLO BOOK
Liz Davis Maxfield
50449652 Book/Online Audio.......... $27.99

JAZZ UKULELE
Abe Lagrimas, Jr.
00121624 Book/Online Audio............$24.99

MUSIC THEORY & EAR TRAINING

BEGINNING EAR TRAINING
Gilson Schachnik
50449548 Book/Online Audio.......... $17.99

BERKLEE CONTEMPORARY MUSIC NOTATION
Jonathan Feist
00202547 Book......................................$24.99

BERKLEE MUSIC THEORY
Paul Schmeling
50449615 Book 1/Online Audio........ $27.99
50449616 Book 2/Online Audio.......$24.99

CONTEMPORARY COUNTERPOINT
Beth Denisch
00147050 Book/Online Audio $24.99

MUSIC NOTATION
Mark McGrain
50449399 Book...................................... $27.99
Matthew Nicholl & Richard Grudzinski
50449540 Book......................................$24.99

REHARMONIZATION TECHNIQUES
Randy Felts
50449496 Book......................................$29.99

CONDUCTING

CONDUCTING MUSIC TODAY
Bruce Hangen
00237719 Book/Online Media $24.99

MUSIC PRODUCTION & ENGINEERING

AUDIO MASTERING
Jonathan Wyner
50449581 Book/CD $34.99

AUDIO POST PRODUCTION
Mark Cross
50449627 Book $27.99

CREATING COMMERCIAL MUSIC
Peter Bell
00278535 Book/Online Media $19.99

HIP-HOP PRODUCTION
Prince Charles Alexander
50449582 Book/Online Audio..........$24.99

THE SINGER-SONGWRITER'S GUIDE TO RECORDING IN THE HOME STUDIO
Shane Adams
00148211 Book $19.99

UNDERSTANDING AUDIO
Daniel M. Thompson
00148197 Book $44.99

MUSIC BUSINESS

CROWDFUNDING FOR MUSICIANS
Laser Malena-Webber
00285092 Book...................................... $17.99

ENGAGING THE CONCERT AUDIENCE
David Wallace
00244532 Book/Online Media..........$16.99

HOW TO GET A JOB IN THE MUSIC INDUSTRY
Keith Hatschek with Breanne Beseda
00130699 Book...................................... $27.99

MAKING MUSIC MAKE MONEY
Eric Beall
00355740 Book $29.99

MUSIC INDUSTRY FORMS
Jonathan Feist
00121814 Book $17.99

MUSIC LAW IN THE DIGITAL AGE
Allen Bargfrede
00366048 Book $24.99

MUSIC MARKETING
Mike King
50449588 Book $24.99

PROJECT MANAGEMENT FOR MUSICIANS
Jonathan Feist
50449659 Book $39.99

THE SELF-PROMOTING MUSICIAN
Peter Spellman
00119607 Book $29.99

ARRANGING & IMPROVISATION

ARRANGING FOR HORNS
Jerry Gates
00121625 Book/Online Audio............$24.99

BERKLEE BOOK OF JAZZ HARMONY
Joe Mulholland & Tom Hojnacki
00113755 Book/Online Audio $29.99

MODERN JAZZ VOICINGS
Ted Pease and Ken Pullig
50449485 Book/Online Audio.......... $27.99

Prices subject to change without notice. Visit your local music dealer or bookstore, or go to **www.berkleepress.com**

SONGWRITING/COMPOSING

BEGINNING SONGWRITING
Andrea Stolpe with Jan Stolpe
00138503 Book/Online Audio...........$22.99

COMPLETE GUIDE TO FILM SCORING
Richard Davis
50449607 Book...................................... $34.99

THE CRAFT OF SONGWRITING
Scarlet Keys
00159283 Book/Online Audio...........$24.99

CREATIVE STRATEGIES IN FILM SCORING
Ben Newhouse
00242911 Book/Online Media............ $27.99

JAZZ COMPOSITION
Ted Pease
50448000 Book/Online Audio $39.99

MELODY IN SONGWRITING
Jack Perricone
50449419 Book......................................$26.99

MUSIC COMPOSITION FOR FILM AND TELEVISION
Lalo Schifrin
50449604 Book......................................$39.99

POPULAR LYRIC WRITING
Andrea Stolpe
50449553 Book $17.99

THE SONGWRITER'S WORKSHOP
Jimmy Kachulis
Harmony
50449519 Book/Online Audio $29.99
Melody
50449518 Book/Online Audio $24.99

SONGWRITING: ESSENTIAL GUIDE
Pat Pattison
Lyric Form and Structure
50481582 Book......................................$19.99
Rhyming
00124366 Book......................................$22.99

SONGWRITING IN PRACTICE
Mark Simos
00244545 Book......................................$16.99

SONGWRITING STRATEGIES
Mark Simos
50449621 Book $27.99

SONGBOOKS

NEW STANDARDS
Terri Lyne Carrington
00369515 Book $29.99

WELLNESS/AUTOBIOGRAPHY

LEARNING TO LISTEN: THE JAZZ JOURNEY OF GARY BURTON
Gary Burton
00117798 Book...................................... $34.99

MANAGE YOUR STRESS AND PAIN THROUGH MUSIC
Dr. Suzanne B. Hanser and Dr. Susan E. Mandel
50449592 Book/Online Audio $34.99

MUSICIAN'S YOGA
Mia Olson
50449587 Book $19.99

NEW MUSIC THERAPIST'S HANDBOOK
Dr. Suzanne B. Hanser
00279325 Book......................................$32.99